"[One] of the best soldiers' memoirs to come out of the 1991 war . . . Joel Turnipseed's *Baghdad Express* shouldn't be overlooked. Like *Jarhead*, it vividly describes what TV viewers didn't see in the last war, or the new one."
—*USA Today*

"At last, book nerds can rejoice. One of our own has returned from war! The military may not miss Joel Turnipseed much, but readers are glad to have him. *Baghdad Express* is a funny, honest, original book."
—Neal Pollack

"This is a coming-of-age story with all the right ingredients: self-deprecation, wit, insight, irony and a lucid enthusiastic writing style."
—*Publishers Weekly*

"The most honest memoir you'll find of real life in the modern military. No stereotype Marines here, just the reality of American men plucked from college, jobs, their wives, and their kids; sometimes scared, sometimes bored, always nervous, and usually in the dark. Turnipseed's story of the Professor and the Dog Pound is a classic of wartime relationships, absurd and funny and sad and true to the casual reader and veteran alike. *Baghdad Express* is a triumph of honesty and humanity."
—Christian Bauman, author of *The Ice Beneath You*

"Turnipseed went to war armed with Plato, Kierkegaard, and a fantastic ear for dialogue. In this singular memoir, Turnipseed weaves philosophical musings with razor-sharp observations of the terror, boredom, and absurdity that was his life during Operation Desert Shield. The result is not just an excellent memoir but a debut of an intriguing new talent."
—*Minneapolis/St. Paul* magazine

"This is the rarest of memoirs—an account of the unglamorous, written with laugh-out-loud dialogue that also reminds us why philosophy matters. Turnipseed has rubbed the jewelry of our philosophic heritage across the touchstone of war and shown which proves true gold and which a shining fraud. He and his Marine comrades in Desert Storm, black and white, deserve our honor and thanks."
—Jonathan Shays, author of *Achilles in Vietnam*

"A deeply felt account of an exile's passage across the back office landscape of modern war. Turnipseed is a lucid, passionate, and oddball observer with an extraordinary ear for vernacular speech and a deft and understated prose style. His book is the best dispatch so far from the Middle East desert battleground." —Alec Wilkinson, author of *My Mentor* and *Big Sugar*

ABOUT THE AUTHOR

Joel Turnipseed served in Operation Desert Shield/Storm in the Sixth Motor Transport Battalion of the United States Marine Corps during the 1990–91 Persian Gulf War. Turnipseed has been a Bread Loaf Scholar, a Writer-in-Residence at The Loft, and a recipient of a Minnesota State Arts Board Fellowship. He lives with his wife in Minneapolis and is at work on a novel.

Baghdad Express

A Gulf War Memoir

Joel Turnipseed

PENGUIN BOOKS

Illustrations by Brian Kelly

This is a work of memory, not of journalism. The names of those who are not my closest friends or family members have been changed to preserve their anonymity and to assure that any errors of memory are charged to me, not them. —Joel Turnipseed

PENGUIN BOOKS
Published by the Penguin Group
Penguin Group (USA) Inc., 375 Hudson Street, New York, New York 10014, U.S.A.
Penguin Books Ltd, 80 Strand, London WC2R 0RL, England
Penguin Books Australia Ltd, 250 Camberwell Road, Camberwell, Victoria 3124, Australia
Penguin Books Canada Ltd, 10 Alcorn Avenue, Toronto, Ontario, Canada M4V 3B2
Penguin Books India (P) Ltd, 11 Community Centre, Panchsheel Park, New Delhi – 110 017, India
Penguin Books (N.Z.) Ltd, Cnr Rosedale and Airborne Roads, Albany, Auckland, New Zealand
Penguin Books (South Africa) (Pty) Ltd, 24 Sturdee Avenue, Rosebank, Johannesburg 2196, South Africa

Penguin Books Ltd, Registered Offices: 80 Strand, London WC2R 0RL, England

First published in the United States of America by Borealis Books,
an imprint of the Minnesota Historical Society Press 2003
Published in Penguin Books 2003

10 9 8 7 6 5 4 3 2 1

Copyright © Joel Turnipseed, 2003
All rights reserved

Quotation from *The Republic* by Plato, translated by Benjamin Jowett (New York: Anchor Books, Double-day, Inc., 1973).

Quotation from *The Gay Science* by Friedrich Nietzsche, translated by Walter Kaufmann (New York: Random House, Inc., 1974).

Quotation from *Seven Pillars of Wisdom* by T. E. Lawrence, copyright 1926, 1935 by Doubleday, a division of Random House, Inc. Used by permission of Doubleday, a division of Random House, Inc.

Quotation of Heraclitus from *Introduction to Metaphysics* by Martin Heidegger, translated by Ralph Manheim, copyright 1959, 1987 by Yale University Press, Inc. Used by permission of Yale University Press, Inc.

The chapter "Being Bombed" originally appeared in *The New York Times Magazine*.

THE LIBRARY OF CONGRESS HAS CATALOGED THE HARDCOVER EDITION AS FOLLOWS:
Turnipseed, Joel, 1968–
Baghdad express : a Gulf War memoir / Joel Turnipseed ; illustrations by Brian Kelly.
p. cm.
ISBN 0-87351-450-5 (hc.)
ISBN 0 14 20.0153 8 (pbk.)
1. Persian Gulf War, 1991—Personal narratives, American.   2. Turnipseed, Joel, 1968–   I. Title.
DS79.74.T87 2003
956.7044'242'092—dc21   2002152053

Printed in the United States of America

Except in the United States of America, this book is sold subject to the condition that it shall not, by way of trade or otherwise, be lent, resold, hired out, or otherwise circulated without the publisher's prior consent in any form of binding or cover other than that in which it is published and without a similar condition including this condition being imposed on the subsequent purchaser.

The scanning, uploading and distribution of this book via the Internet or via any other means without the permission of the publisher is illegal and punishable by law. Please purchase only authorized electronic editions, and do not participate in or encourage electronic piracy of copyrighted materials. Your support of the author's rights is appreciated.

A philosophy should be portable.

Paul Valéry, Journals

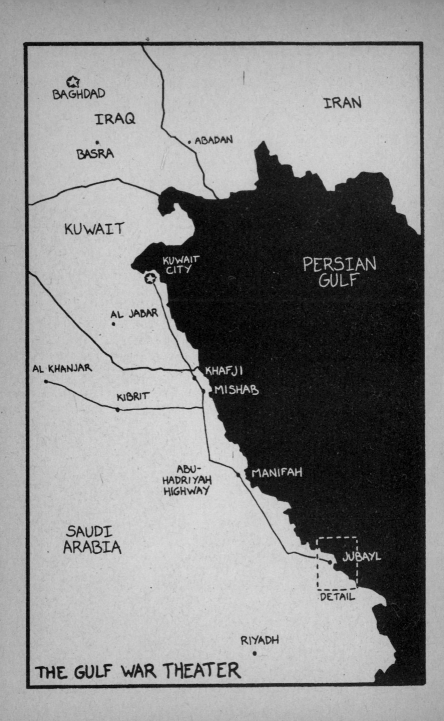

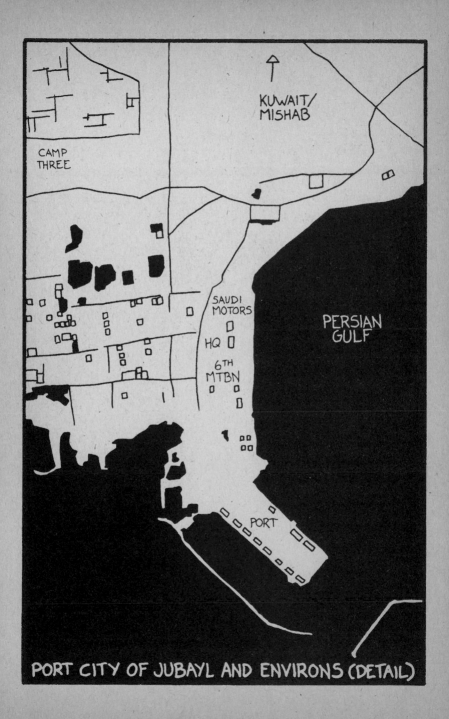

PORT CITY OF JUBAYL AND ENVIRONS (DETAIL)

EVERYTHING PASSED QUICKLY, like the shadows of the sparse clouds sailing over the California desert. We stepped from the rubber-matted stairs of the Marine Corps bus to the sticky asphalt of Norton Air Force Base. Reflexively, we raised our hands in salute—to nobody in particular; to the sun. It was mid-afternoon on January 17, the morning after the war started.

We had gotten up early, packed our gear, and put the finishing touches on our ALICE packs and our H-harnesses: flashlights and Ka-Bar fighting knives and entrenching tools and ammo pouches and canteens and first-aid kits buckled and snapped and duct-taped in their places on nylon straps clipped to a cartridge belt, forming an H over our bodies. We checked our chemical weapons gear and gas masks. We cleaned our M-16's. We dressed for the first time in our desert camouflage uniforms, which we called "chocolate chips." We were all reservists activated as truck drivers, but the Corps' mission states that every Marine is a combat warrior.

After breakfast the day before, we had filed into a movie theater on Camp Pendleton. The screen was raised, and the only prop on the stage was a stand with a microphone. Several staff and gunnery sergeants paced the aisles while we waited. Then we heard footsteps from the wings, beating out the quick-clipped rhythms of war. A balding, six-foot colonel burst onto the stage, grabbing the microphone from its stand while still in stride, like Wayne Newton doing Patton.

"Good morning, Marines!" he said.

"Morning, sir."

"First day of a goddam war and you can't say good goddam morning? I said, 'Good morning, Marines!'"

"Morning, sir!"

"Ooh-Rah, I just got a hard-on. Now, you ladies and gentlemen are sitting here before me wondering why I'm talking about war," said the colonel, breaking into a falsetto: "But it's just the deadline, sir." He paused. "Bullshit. Sodom Insane is not going to back down, and neither are we. Why? 'Cause he's a crazy goddam Ay-rab and we're the United States Marine Corps."

A lone voice called out from the crowd, "We're gonna kick some Iraqi ass, sir."

"What'd you say?" asked the colonel.

The guy stood up, about thirty rows back. "We're gonna kick some Iraqi ass, sir."

"Any of these other limp dicks gonna help, or are you gonna win the Medal of Honor all by your lonesome?" said the colonel. "What are the rest of you sorry excuses for Marines going to do?"

"Kick some Iraqi ass, sir."

"What?"

"Kick some Iraqi ass, sir."

"I'm afraid my tired old ass is going to have to retire, cause I just plain can't hear you ladies."

"KICK SOME IRAQI ASS, SIR."

"Goddam, I love this shit," said the colonel. "Gotta get my ass over there to fight alongside you Marines." He lowered his head for a moment. "Seriously, now, I need to let you in on some vital intelligence. Barring the interference of God, we are going to be at war when you ladies and gentlemen hit the sands of Saudi Arabia. Frankly, I think even God wants the Marines to go kick some Iraqi ass, with a ringside seat at the Mother of All Battles."

He paused again, lowering the microphone to his waist. When he spoke again, he was earnest, avuncular.

"I gotta be honest with you, Marines. You are going to be driving trucks to hell. Oil fires. Bodies. Bad shit. And on the way to getting his ass kicked all the way back to almighty Allah, Sodom's going to take the lives of thirty percent of the Marines coming at him. That's right, *thirty percent*. And you gentlemen are going to be driving tractor-trailers, driving the broad side of a barn through a weapons range. Take a minute to look to your left, then look to your right. One of the three of you is coming home in a box with a Purple Heart and a folded flag."

We did as he said, and thought, "Sorry fucker next to me ain't comin' back."

Then he was back at his schtick: "Are you afraid? Goddam right you are. Is that going to prevent you from carrying out the glorious tradition of our beloved Corps? Hell, no. You are the best-trained, best-equipped Marines ever to step foot on a battlefield. You have the utmost love and support of your country and your God. You are motivated, dedicated, die-hard, ass-kicking, sand-busting, Saddam-hating, fearless, brass-balled, spit-polished, de-luxe, hi-tech, combat warriors. Tomorrow you will be in Saudi Arabia. You will be at war. Semper Fi, Marines."

We had flown to Camp Pendleton the week before, on January 11. My mother and I got up at five that day, after staying up until two. It was a cold morning in Minneapolis, the snow crisp and deep blue in the moonlight. My mother's only advice to me on the drive to the airport was, "Keep the enemies on the other side, all right?"

Mom. We sat quietly for the rest of the drive. The sun was just coming up as we walked to the terminal. We were alone as we walked, passed only by the occasional red-eyed passenger or airport employee steering a yellow cart.

Of the thirty or so Marines scheduled for the flight, only about half had arrived when my mother and I showed up. Clouds of smoke rose from the cigarettes of the nervous. Fathers and sons and wives began showing up in small groups, now chatting, now silently pacing. By the time the pale light of morning filled the waiting area, it was standing room only. We were flying in civilian clothes, but you could tell the

Marines by their haircuts: zero at the ear and collar, fading up to no more than three inches on top—jarheads. Wives and husbands and mothers and children were crying, calling out, "Over here!" to arriving friends. I did the same.

"Well," my friend Maggie said as we hugged, "make sure you're home in time for the wedding."

"If I have to go AWOL," I said.

"That should be no problem," she said.

Then I turned to Mark, my best friend. We both reached out, then hugged silently with one hand clasped and the other around a shoulder. Sarah, my—and what the hell was she, exactly? We had kissed once, tentatively—was standing next to us, rocking on her heels. She was beautiful but fragile—a ballerina. We had just met. We shared an awkward hug, then turned away.

A minute later I was swept up in the rush of bodies boarding a 727 for California en route to the Persian Gulf. When the plane was over Arizona, the captain polled us on the intercom, asking how many of us had seen the Grand Canyon. A few hands went up, and the flight attendant disappeared behind the cockpit door. Suddenly the plane flipped on its side, perpendicular to the ground.

"If you look down to your right, Marines, you'll see the most glorious land in America, the Grand Canyon. I'm going to run the length of the canyon, then pull around so the other half of you can see it. It'd be a shame to die without being allowed to see this."

We could hear the air traffic controller yelling at the pilot, telling him to return to his flight plan.

"What the hell does he know?" the pilot asked us. "He ain't going to war."

The pilot turned a figure 8, and for the next five minutes, I looked straight down into the Grand Canyon.

At Norton Air Force Base, we walked briskly beneath the C-5 cargo transport plane, dropping our seabags on pallets lying in its shadow. We headed for a low-slung cinder-block building attached to the hangars, its industrial steel doors held open with orange highway cones. Inside, folding chairs were haphazardly aligned, and we dropped haphazardly into them, our arms draping over the backs, our legs splayed out before us. Some men sprawled out in sleep along the cinder-block walls, or curled up like children, embracing their rifles with the butt between their thighs and the barrel cradled in their arms. None of us had slept much the night before.

We had less than a week to prepare for war. Our first day was a roving, shuffling clusterfuck. The Minneapolis bus was the first to arrive at Camp Pendleton from LAX. Then came buses carrying reservists from Dallas and Memphis and Green Bay, Philadelphia and Whidbey Island, Washington. Long lines of Marines sauntering off the buses in civilian clothes, looking at their new surroundings with the wonder of children: men leaning over balconies, appearing on rooftops, climbing trees, gathering in circles. Then we formed into squads by reserve unit. We hurried. We waited. Finally, our Staff NCOs passed word that the barracks were still locked up, and we scattered across the grounds.

I sat beneath a tree, decked out in khakis, white oxford and dark-green cardigan, wearing gold and tortoise-shell glasses. I smoked my pipe and tried to look philosophical, holding a fountain pen over a blank page of my journal. The other Marines threw rocks and footballs at each other, smoking and joking.

At noon someone drove up to open the barracks. Drawn by instinct from our scatter around the grounds, we collected our things and thoughts, stubbed our cigarettes, and shuffled into formation—forty inches back to chest, four inches shoulder to shoulder: Marines standing at attention.

Inside the barracks, we barely had time to drop our seabags on our bunks before we got started: chow, then processing. We put new filters in our gas masks while listening to lectures on nuclear, biological, and chemical weapons. We checked out chemical weapons suits, traded our old green uniforms for new green uniforms and desert camouflage. We signed reams of paper. We double-, then triple-checked our first-aid kits. We took roll call about a dozen times. It was just days before President Bush's January 15 deadline for war with Iraq.

When we got our liberty, I tossed my newly issued chemical weapons suits and uniforms in my locker, then walked out to the rusted stairs of the barracks fire escape. The sun lit up the sky like a Grateful Dead T-shirt; it had just disappeared behind the slopes separating us from the Pacific coast. I pulled my pipe and pouch from my shirt pocket, rolling a wad of tobacco to tamp, then light, then tamp, then smoke, all in a familiar, reassuring order.

The dull clunk of metal stairs rang beneath my feet. Behind me, men wandered from bunk to bunk, discussing their preparations for war and a night at the Enlisted Club.

Below me, a voice called, "Smokin' a pipe, huh, Turnip?" It was Solter, one of the guys from Minneapolis.

"How'd you guess?"

"I smelled it. Reminded me of my grandpa. You thinking about that philosophy stuff?"

"You didn't smell that, too, did you?"

"Just figured. You going to the E-Club?"

"No, I'm gonna hit the rack early tonight. You?"

"I don't know. I better call my wife. She's worried we're gonna go to war."

"Well, we are, aren't we?"

"You think?"

"You ever hear the words *Remember the Maine?*"

"In school or something. I forget."

"They mean *We're going to war whether you like it or not, so don't fuck with us.* Tell your wife you're going to war, Solter."

I felt like an asshole. I was an asshole. Still, there was no doubt we were going to war. There was no use lying about it. Half an hour later, Bush was on television, informing the American people.

* * *

The deadline had passed the night before we bused to Norton AFB, but we still hadn't heard if a war had been declared. Now we watched the logistics guys tool around on their dollies, loading our plane. The wire-reinforced plate glass of the hangar lobby superimposed, over this activity, the shadows of USO volunteers handing out cold pizza and flat cola. All women, they wore a uniform of red-stained apron, white perm, white sneakers and discount blue jeans. Their bloodshot eyes were swollen with purple bags. The smell of aviation fuel permeated the lobby, beyond which we could see the C-5 that would take us to war. The women stood behind the fold-out church-basement table, now serving a single Marine. As he walked back to his seat, one of them followed, reaching up to turn on the lobby television.

The soft click, then the sharp crack of static, brought the listless to life: CNN exploded onto the screen, sending a riot alert through our nervous systems. Anti-aircraft fire and flares lit up the Baghdad skies, and sirens screamed beneath the rumble of bombs. The men who had been sleeping on the floor began queuing up at the two pay telephones, and the first few rows of seats filled with men craning their necks backward, eyes glued to the spectacle. Above the quiet shuffle of Marines shaking off sleep in a lobby at Norton Air Force Base in California, someone said, "Fuckin' A, we're going to war." Nobody Ooh-Rah'd.

Our flight to Saudi Arabia stopped over in Torrejon, Spain. As we stepped down the steel ramp, emerging from the belly of the C-5, we saw endless giant forms shrouded in a moonless midnight fog, a dense whiteness illuminated by sparsely placed halogen lamps, swirling flood-lights, and the rotating orange and red lights of row upon row of B-52 bombers and C-5 cargo transports.

Inside the hangar serving as a transit barracks, everybody was watching CNN. I joined the crowd, still carrying my ALICE pack (a rabbit hole we were most definitely headed down, but this ALICE was "All-Purpose Lightweight Individual Carrying Equipment"). Huddled around the televisions in two corners were U.S. Army Rangers, National Guardsman, and Marines; British Army and Marines; and some Canadians, all with eyes fastened on the screens. Staccato flashes of anti-aircraft tracers flying in every direction out of Baghdad. Reporters giving dispatches with sirens blaring in the background. Then we learned about Iraqi SCUDS landing in Israel. Larry Register in Jerusalem, holding a phone at a cluttered desk, being wired for sound by a guy wearing a gas mask. Lou Dobbs asking him to point the camera out the window. Sirens wailing.

"Fucking Israel, man," someone said.

"Fucking Israel," we agreed.

Wolf Blitzer at the Pentagon, confirming a SCUD landing. *". . . a massive Israeli reaction from the air force, the Israeli Air Force, which has been bracing all day for this kind of attack."*

"War's over, boys," one of the Rangers said. "Baghdad's gonna be a glass parking lot before we leave this hangar."

Richard Roth in Tel Aviv. *"We're just listening to explosions."*

Shaky camera shots, then cut to the studio. I sat on my pack and chain smoked, ashing on the floor like everyone else. Scenes from Dahran, Riyadh, Jerusalem, Tel Aviv, Washington, and Atlanta flickered in the blue haze. Wolf Blitzer again.

"Obviously this rewrites all the equations for this war."

"War, shit pal, Israeli Air Force gonna end this thing by mornin' chow."

"We know now that Israel is going to retaliate, if it already hasn't started. The Israeli sources here in Washington tell us that the Israeli Air Force will undertake a massive retaliatory strike."

Charles Jaco in Saudi Arabia. *"Okay, guys, break it down. Out of here!"*

Cut to Israeli police officer standing in a pile of rubble in Tel Aviv. *"What can I say to you? War—it is not a summer camp."*

From the Pentagon, Wolf Blitzer says that despite conflicting reports, it is believed that no chemical or biological warheads were on the SCUDS, eight of which hit Israel. He's doing voice-over to a live feed from Saudi Arabia, with sirens screaming in the background. *"Planes are taking off from an air base in Saudi Arabia."*

Tweaked-out screen, then distortion, then cut to Blitzer. *"We lost our feed."*

CNN—we were so tuned in they had a direct coax link to our cerebral cortex: a chain-smoking war borg in a Mediterranean hangar. SCUDS in Tel Aviv. CNN. Electric night in Baghdad. CNN. Sirens in Dahran. CNN. Generals with wicked in-flight video in Riyadh. CNN, giving new meaning to "theater of war."

The webbed canvas seats of a C-5 are small and crowded, and face the rear of the plane. Now into the second day of our journey, somewhere over the Mediterranean, most of the guys slept. Unable to sleep, I meandered through Plato's *Republic*, using a pink Hi-Liter to mark the passages that would change my life:

> *A man must take with him into the world below an adamantine faith in truth and right, that there too he may be undazzled by the desire of wealth or other allurements of evil, lest, coming upon tyrannies and other villainies, he do irremediable wrongs to others and suffer yet worse himself; but let him know how to choose the mean and avoid the extremes on either side, as far as possible, not only in this life but in all that which is to come. For this is the way of happiness.*

Our Staff NCOs, Boomer and Landers, appeared at the head of the stairs, carrying satchels. We had MRES in our ALICE packs, so they weren't serving the in-flight meal.

A snack?

"Heads up, Marines. We're going to be passing out rounds. Three hundred and sixty per Marine. We want you to put twenty in each magazine. I know they hold thirty, but you'll trash the spring, so don't fill 'em up. Put the rest of the rounds in the bottom of your ALICE pack. And don't lose any rounds—you gotta turn these in when we come home."

Nothing quite like a couple hundred Marine reservists, cramped ass-hole to elbow on a cargo plane, suddenly pulling out M-16's and filling magazines with 5.56 mm NATO rounds. Someone yelled out behind me, "Fly the friendly skies, motherfuckers! The Corps is coming downrange."

Every Marine is a combat warrior. I don't remember his exact occupa-tional specialty, but my Senior Drill Instructor in boot camp was some-thing like a Marine Corps postal worker. Even so, he could drop your ass in a heartbeat. A badass, black-belt mailman. That's the Marines. Chesty Puller, the most decorated Marine in history. Smedley Butler, author of *War Is a Racket* and the only Marine to win the Medal of Honor twice. Lee Harvey Oswald. Charles Whitman—who shot and killed fourteen people from a tower at the University of Texas; whose father literally beat him into the Marine Corps. Every last one of us field-stripped and rebuilt from the ground up at Marine Corps Recruit Depot; every last one of us could turn out to be a hero with titanium balls; every last one of us stood an equal chance of turning into a psychotic with a steady trigger finger and a firing pin trained to our pulse.

Back at Camp Pendleton, in the haste of checking out gear and get-ting our shots, we managed a day at the rifle range. I loved the cadences of the rifle range—long days of pulling targets or waiting to fire. Two hundred meters. Three hundred meters. Five hundred meters. To think: I could hit a dog target, Marine Corps nomenclature for a human sil-houette, nine times out of ten in the black from more than a quarter-mile—without a scope. I watched the guys raise the targets above the slow rolling fog on the grass. The sun was just coming up beyond the berm, a six-foot wall of brown sod. Soon its horizion would be dotted with white canvases glued with targets.

"Ready on your left, ready on your right . . . all ready on the firing line. Shooters, you may commence firing when your dog target appears."

I could feel the pebbles on the asphalt firing line; feel my pulse in the sling of my rifle. I switched focus from the end of my nose to a quarter-mile away, triangulating the rear sight of my rifle, the grey dot in the distance, and the front sight, on which I focused as I eased my body into its routine: Breathe, Relax, Aim, Stop, Squeeze.

"Cease fire! Cease fire! Unload, clear, and lock!"

More than five football fields away, a spotter marked a bull. And then there were the burnt rounds. Their nitrate-laden smoke smells like both death and childhood—somewhere between burnt flesh and the caps I shot as a kid. Unquestionably there was a romance to this—but also a kind of insanity.

It seemed like I could still smell the firing range, sitting in my cramped seat on the C-5. When I got tired of reading, I quietly slung my rifle over my shoulder, then descended to the open bulkhead below. My boots banged a dull, metallic chord on the planks running the length of the cargo bay. I marveled that I could walk in a flying cavern. Pallets stacked with our seabags, wrapped in nylon webbing, rested in a corner by several plywood crates stenciled with serial numbers and unit designations. Two mine-sweepers were chained down in the middle of the bay: heavy-tracked tanks with bulldozer blades made of steel thicker than my fist, steel whose deflecting curves rose to a blunt edge just beneath my eyes. I walked over to one and ran my fingers along the blade's cold surface, its imperceptibly pebbled smoothness and invincible solidity.

At the far end of the bay, I climbed a steep stairwell to the short hallway between the cockpit and the officers' deck. The crew chief rose from his seat just outside the officers' deck.

"I'll take your rifle, Marine."

"It's still open, then?" I asked. "The offer to hang out in the cockpit?"

"Yeah, just can't let you take your rifle in there," he replied, "for the obvious reasons."

"Hijackers?" I asked.

"No, it's real crowded in there. What the fuck?"

I opened the door just enough to squeeze through, and crouched behind the navigator's chair. All the pilots were leaning back, chatting, while the plane flew itself.

"Evening, gentlemen," I said.

"Evening, Marine," called the captain. "Enjoying the flight? Not too rough, is it?"

We had flown through some serious turbulence, and must have jumped the cliff between a high and low pressure front, because we felt at one point like we were not only losing our cookies, but gravity as well. Hitting the wall on the other side had knocked us out of our seats.

"Yeah, that was great," I said, "really great. When everyone was done barfing, someone had the balls to yell, 'One more for Chesty!'"

"You point him out, and we'll have him scrub the deck when we land in Jubayl. What can I do for you this evening?"

We talked about flying a C-130, which I had done while enrolled in Marine Corps Platoon Leaders Class. Then we talked about ophthalmology: eye exercises to correct vision impairment, the problems of red-green color blindness and instrument panels: we went through the whole deck—the major and minor arcana of eyesight.

"You know, even though you wear glasses, you can still be a navigator," offered the navigator, sporting a pair of black-framed military issue glasses cocked above his goofy smile. I was reminded why we called them BCGS: birth-control glasses.

"So where are we, anyway?"

"We're about a hundred miles off the coast of Egypt right now. If you look out, off to the right here, you'll be able to make out Alex."

"Alexandria? They used to have the world's greatest library."

"Library? Ain't gonna be a library where you're headed, Marine." The navigator looked over at the captain, raising his eyebrows.

The instrument panels and cabin lights lit the windows with our reflections, and I struggled to stare through the dark to a luminous patch of earth that was barely visible.

"I don't need a library," I said, "I brought my own. Half a seabag full of books."

Everyone in the cockpit turned to look at me.

"That's great, Marine. They'll probably come in real handy, like when you build a bunker out of them."

We all laughed, then ceased abruptly. I stood behind the pilots for several more minutes, quietly gazing out the window, mesmerized by the unchanging darkness before us.

Footsteps

WHAT WAS SADDAM HUSSEIN THINKING? What was I thinking? Mostly, in those days, I was thinking about philosophy, deep inside the fire, walking around campus with a thousand-yard stare. When I wasn't thinking about philosophy, I was looking for a place to live. Everything else was optional: futon, rice bowl, pens, journals, books—that was it. I didn't even own a bicycle.

I was first activated in August, within weeks of Saddam's invasion of Kuwait. I had just moved in with my Minneapolis buddy Dave, with whom I'd joined the Marines out of high school. We were both studying at the U, and now we were both activated, assigned to a few weeks at Marine Corps Air Station, Cherry Point, North Carolina. Dave went down as a cook, and I went down as an advanced automotive mechanic. There wasn't much advanced to our job there, which was to dress the shop queens—skeletons of trucks that had been stripped for parts to get the rest of their vehicles ready to ship. Our shop chief pointed at a pallet of parts, pointed toward the carcasses of five-ton trucks, and said, "Put those parts on these here trucks." So we did, from nine to five every day. After hours I played cribbage with Dave, and spent time flipping channels between CNN and local coverage of the Helms-Gant Senate race.

Then, in September, I came home.

A week or so before Christmas, Dave was activated again and sent to flip burgers at Marine Corps Air Station, El Toro, California.

Just after the New Year I had been sitting in a Minneapolis coffee shop with my pal Mark. Through slow-rising whorls of smoke, I watched the students on the streets below trudging, bundled and stooped, through the campus gates. Mark and I sat at our corner table.

Here the art and the conversation were equally striving and derivative, but at least they were ours. We had been sitting at this table for years, seemed like, debating points for our papers or op-ed pieces to the *Minnesota Daily*, talking philosophy and politics and religion, playing Go— an ancient Chinese game with simple rules that unfold into mind-bending complexity as the game progresses. Other times we simply sat and drank black coffee and stared out the window in silence, sloughing off the ennui of winter days. On that day, we were talking about war.

"Suppose you get the call?" asked Mark. "What then?"

I hesitated. "You know what old Henry has to say, 'Emulate the philosopher and walk out the gate empty-handed.'"

Mark's great value as a friend, and an intellect, was his clear-sighted patience, a willingness to press things gently, with a smile, and never into a corner. He asked, "What does old Joel have to say? I mean, is the yachtsman's rule in effect?"

The yachtsman's rule: make a list of only those things absolutely essential for the journey—then cut it in half. I didn't know if he meant it literally or metaphorically.

"Well," I answered, "I'm only sitting in on classes, which I'll register for if I'm not called up. As for the place, Maggie's already moving her stuff out, so I'm looking around for rooms now. I'm definitely traveling light."

The fact was, I had no clue where I would live if I *didn't* get called up.

When I arrived home, I trudged up the stairs to where a lone bulb shed its underclass light on my apartment's deadbolt. Until Dave got activated just before Christmas, he, his fiancée, Maggie, and I had shared this squalid two-bedroom apartment on Franklin Avenue, where we put leftovers out by the dumpsters for the bums and answered questions the police asked us when the woman downstairs got raped, or when one of the Somali women stabbed her husband. Now that Dave was gone, Maggie was moving in with her parents. My lease was up.

The living room was all but empty—a few plastic milk crates strewn haphazardly across the cream-colored carpet. A black-and-white TV blinked blue heads. I walked to the kitchen. I tossed the latest eviction notice from the counter, then peered reflexively into the empty refrigerator. The phone rang.

"Is Lance Corporal Turnipseed there?"

"I guess this means I haven't been promoted again," I answered.

"This is Staff Sergeant Dix. Have you got a pen?"

"No."

"Get one. Tomorrow morning you will report to drill at zero-seven-thirty, you will report at zero-seven-thirty on Sunday. You have Monday and Tuesday to conduct personal affairs, and at zero-seven-thirty Wednesday you become an active-duty Marine. Do you have anything that needs to be stored?"

I paused to look out at the empty living room.

"Right now?" I asked. Irony had evidently ridden the wrong bus, felt lost, abused and ridiculous, standing naked before a hostile audience, before Staff Sergeant Dix.

He didn't need to know and we parted company. My relationship with the Marine Corps had been rather tenuous for several years, including most recently a period of separation. Some people even talked of desertion. Basically, it was UA—Unauthorized Absence, what the Marine Corps calls AWOL, my status for four months in the spring. I didn't want to be a Marine anymore. So I didn't go to reserve drills.

When I first stood on the yellow footprints at Marine Corps Recruit Depot, San Diego, the only thing about them for which I hadn't been prepared from birth was their forty-five degree angle: I was pigeon-toed. It took me half of boot camp to figure out what Drill Instructor Sergeant Ratliff was getting at when he yelled, "Kick the ball, Turnipseed. Kick the damned ball—like a soccer player." For a guy who made no bones about our faults, it struck me as odd that he never just flat-out said, "Turnipseed—point your toes at forty-five degrees, like the yellow footprints, you pigeon-toed fuck."

Marching skills aside, I was a dream recruit: messed up enough that I had nowhere else to go; smart and aggressive enough to want to prove something. In the end, I walked across the stage wearing an extra stripe on my sleeve, an honor graduate.

It had been downhill from there: whenever the conflict between the ideal and the actual nature of the Marine Corps manifested itself, I longed for the ideal. When *esprit de corps* meant "promote your buddy," when *Semper Fi* meant "unless you're black, or you make me look like a fat slob on the physical fitness test, or my ass could be on the line," I increasingly blamed the Marine Corps and not the Marines.

Now that I was in college, I wanted to be a philosopher and sit in the coffee shop and talk Kierkegaard. If I wanted to take a two-week trip somewhere, it would be San Francisco or Manhattan—not a high-desert air-strip at Twenty-Nine Palms or mosquito-infested Camp Ripley in northern Minnesota. After several attempts to enlighten me, including a rather interesting debate that ranged over Plato's *Republic* and the Uniform Code of Military Justice, our co sent me a letter offering me a general discharge. If I signed I was out; if I had the least shred of spine or sense of honor, I could make up my drills and stay a Marine. I almost signed. Instead, I spent a couple weeks in May and June fixing the transmission and transfer case on a five-ton truck. In August, Saddam Hussein invaded Kuwait, on implicit reassurance by the United States that this would be cool. There was no going back for either of us. Who knows, perhaps Foreign Service officers were on the phone to Baghdad, falsely assuaging Saddam's fears, at the very hour one or another of the Marine Corps' officers was assuaging mine.

In the end, as it was in the beginning, the Corps was all I had.

After hanging the phone back on the wall, I walked over to our living room window and gazed at the street below. It was now covered with a blanket of light snow and long shadows, and the streets and cars below seemed magical, haunting. I stood silently in the drapeless windows, hands by my sides, thinking . . . white static thoughts about nothing in particular.

I walked back into the kitchen to make phone calls. No one home. Not Mark, not Sarah, not my mother, not my grandparents, neither my brother nor my sister, and Maggie was shuttling between our fast-emptying apartment and her parents' attic, overflowing with the drift-stuff of three kids in college. There was no way I was calling my father. After walking aimlessly into the living room, I sat down on a milk crate.

"Fuck.

"This is fucked.

"I'm fucked. This fucking sucks. What the fuck?"

I went through the entire grammar of "fuck," then gave the fuck up. How do you tell an answering machine that you're going to war?

I went to the TV and turned up the volume, then changed the channel, and there's some high school debate team member talking about how we need to "take care of this guy, Saddam." I felt like I was being sent to war by a kid. I turned the channel again, and Ron Kovac was shouting through a bullhorn. This was cool enough in its way, but I wasn't sure that we shouldn't be kicking Saddam's ass. I definitely did not feel like I could cruise to Canada for this war. I turned off the television.

I had to escape the barrenness of the apartment, which, given the recent rapid acceleration of my personal history, had come to seem less a metaphorical than literal bare prison cell. I descended the dark stairs again to go for a walk. Outside, I realized that it was bitterly cold, and that the threateningly austere light cast on the bicarbonate snow was too harsh, anyway, to meditate under. I force marched to the hostile crunch of a January sidewalk towards the Holiday convenience store.

Having come for nothing in particular, I walked idly through the aisles, singing a Clash tune to myself: *Lost in the Supermarket*. I walked past 10w30, past Skittles, shuffled past notions and potions and lotions. I felt empty, pathetic. My first act after learning I was going to war was to head for a gas station to buy pretzels and a Coke with my last dimes and nickels? Fuck that. I tossed them back onto the steel rack of chips and walked to the counter.

I looked at the stoner behind the register and said, "Gimme a pack of cigarettes." I didn't even smoke.

"Uh, any particular brand?" he asked.

I felt like a complete asshole. "Camels," I said.

"Yeah?" He had me, and his bloodshot eyes registered the kill. "What kind you lookin' for? Straights? Filters? Lights? Hard pack? What?" he asked in quick succession, as though I would go down for the count, or confess under the bare-knuckled pressure.

"Straights," I replied, leaning back against the magazine rack. This seemed to satisfy him. After depositing what remained of my wealth on the dirty counter I stepped back out into the snow-and-fume-filled night. Once clear of the plate glass of the Holiday station, I struck my matches clumsily in the falling snow, shivering in the half-protection of the bus shelter to achieve the dim cherry glow of my first cigarette.

This awkwardness, this abruptness, was not new to me: I was born into it. When my father got tired of beating my mother, he moved out of our trailer. I was two. There followed a succession of years whose only constant was change: from the trailer to student housing at the University of Illinois, and then to Duluth. When my mother had a nervous breakdown, my little brother Mike and I were shipped to Little Chute, Wisconsin. Then, when my stepmother could no longer stand me, I was shipped singleton to Burnsville, Minnesota. My mother decided I was still too much and shipped me back to Little Chute, where I learned that I had taken second place in the fourth-grade science fair. I moved with my father and stepmother to East Duluth for seventh grade, then out to West Duluth for eighth grade. Then my middle school closed and I bused to a new school for ninth grade. When I broke the paddle my stepmother intended to spank me with, I went back to my mother, now living in suburban Minneapolis. In all, I went to a different school in a different city every year from kindergarten to tenth grade. It made me a connoisseur of loneliness.

Because I had no one to show me who or how to be, I looked for it everywhere—and desperately. If it's possible to be a fifth-grade nihilist, that would have been me: trying on the style of *Saturday Night Live* skits; aping Elvis Costello on my uncle Dave's reel-to-reel; staying up late at my grandparents' place in Connecticut, reading my uncle Howard's copies of *Mad* magazine, *The Anarchist's Cookbook*, and more esoteric leaflets and 'zines from hippie communes—where the guys all smoked weed and the chicks walked around with nothing but a bandolier covering their breasts, holding a baby in one hand and a Kalishnikov in the other.

I was a total freak.

I had nightmares all through my youth about running from an exploding car. Just flat-fuck streaking down a highway in the middle of nowhere. I told my mother about these dreams once when I was a teenager.

"Those weren't nightmares," she said. "Your father left me with the payments on the trailer and a 1963 Pontiac. One day, when I was driving you and Mikey to daycare, it caught on fire. I had to drag you and carry Mikey across the highway before it burst into flames."

I took to philosophy to build, brick by unassailable brick, a bunker of truth, inside of which I could work on the greater labor of building an unassailable happiness. This was the only thing that mattered—and I had a sense, heading to war, that I would somehow complete this task in the desert, where wisdom had always been achieved.

I spent my last night as a civilian at my mother's place. The snow teemed like white bugs against Mark's windshield for the entire long, silent, thirty-five-mile drive out to her new-rich fantasy—"The Farm" that she shared with my stepfather, Bill: five acres of apple, hawthorne, cherry, willow, oak and pine trees. A half-acre garden. Fence posts with dangling fallen rails. A rope swing hanging from the gnarled and ancient arm of a willow out front, down the gentle slope from the porch that surrounded two sides of the house. All covered in a thick blanket of snow and darkness. It was already late when Mark came to pick me up, and it was getting later as we drove over fast-gaining drifts. The radio was off and all things culminated in silence. A silence in which the purr of the engine and susurrous run of wheels over slush intruded only at the margins.

After a brief handshake and a pop of the trunk, Mark left me to a last night with family. It definitely wasn't home. I sighed deeply as I stood before the door, green seabags stacked at my sides. I stepped into another world when I crossed the threshold: one of stenciled ivy borders, potpourri, brass teakettles, oak trim, well-polished oak floors, faux-country painted cows, and faux-feelings.

The evening's enjoyment mostly turned on the banal, and in this instance culminated in my dressing up for war: donning the camouflage utilities, the H-harness from which my canteens and ammunition pouches and first-aid kit and knife and flashlight hung, and my ALICE pack. A gas mask was slung across one hip, my flak jacket and helmet on my chest and skull. I dressed in the privacy of the library, wishing to surprise everyone with the sudden transformation. As I changed from philosopher to warrior, I glanced at the shelves, newly filled with my books—my prized editions of Emerson and Thoreau, the turn-of-the-century Houghton Mifflin editions in blue cloth, a two-hundred-year-old Gibbon in twelve volumes, as well as dozens and dozens of philosophy and classics titles from the Cambridge and Oxford University Presses. All were out of place and jam-packed on shelves that used to accommodate *National Geographic*s, woodworking manuals, and management how-to's. When I glanced at the books on the bottom rows, I laughed at my feet—I was still wearing my argyle socks, which matched the spines of the Princeton Kierkegaard volumes with their colorful greens and reds and blues against black. Boots, of course, were strictly prohibited on the lush carpets.

I straightened myself and called into the living room, "Okay, are you ready?"

"Don't come out yet!" my mother cried cheerfully. "I've got to wait for the flash to warm up!" With her in the living room were my brother, Mike, my sister, Carrie, and my stepfather, Bill.

I looked down at a new leather-bound book lying on the library table. It had been distressed to look like a Gutenberg, thick with pages. It was entitled simply "Family." Our genealogy. I opened it to ancient sepia portraits and documents from the old world, and the new world in its infancy. I turned toward the present, flipping pages while my family talked in the living room. When I came to my mother's page, on which my information had been posted, I ran down it quickly, noting the words I'd submitted in self-description and—

"Okay! You can come out now!" yelled my mother. But my head jerked away even before she called out.

I paused, face red, pulse beating in my neck, pulse throbbing in the catgut tightness of my chest. My voice fumbled as I searched for an excuse, a reason to pause and collect myself. I bit the inside of my cheek, drawing blood, and took a deep breath. "Fuck this," I muttered, just barely under my breath. Foolishly, with little care and less wisdom, someone had entered the name of my biological father—yes, I knew it already, I am a *bastard*, born a palimpsest: adopted and renamed before my first breath. When my mother got knocked up by a guy at a party, and he refused to have anything to do with her afterwards, my father led my uncles in beating the crap out of the guy. He seemed like a hero to her.

My father—nominal, not biological, about whom no more—had run away from his parents in Gary, Indiana; running from drunkenness, profanity, and the fiery despair brought home from the steel mills. He ended up in boot camp and then, right in the middle of that new version of hell, just up and walked away. I've heard drunken tales of fist-swinging getaways, but know only that he ended up in Duluth using an assumed name, as a roadie and hanger-on with my uncles' rock band. At that time my grandmother lived in a giant white house in Duluth, with pillars and gargoyles in front, and she worked as an ad writer and editor at the CBS radio and television affiliate. She had studied English and humanities at the University of Minnesota, one of the great programs of its time, headed by Warren Beach. Allen Tate, Saul Bellow, John Berryman, and Robert Penn Warren all made their way through as professors in the postwar years. My mother and uncles and their family must have seemed damned attractive to my father, more so even than the safety of Canada just a few hundred miles away.

My uncle Tom headed for Canada. I think he stayed until Carter gave him a pardon and spent his first couple years back in the United States in rehab. Chuck, the leader of the band, was drafted. He was granted Conscientious Objector status and made an MP at Cam Ranh Bay.

My parents moved me to southside Chicago. After a few months, they moved again to the cornfields of Urbana, Illinois, and a nice, comfy double-wide.

It would be painful enough to say, "And those were the golden years, when I looked up to him." But standing there in the library, I was shot through with the pain of knowing he'd begun to fuck up even then: when my grandmother gave him a job, still on the lam and using an alias, he'd used his *real* social security number on the paperwork, and ended up spending my mother's pregnancy in jail in Colorado.

When Bill asked, "Aren't you coming?" I smiled. I really did, and walked around the corner into the living room, looking and feeling like a ridiculous human insect in my body armor and gas mask.

"A *Metamorphosis!*" I said, stepping out into the living room. I felt a profound sadness, humor and melancholy mixing like beer and wine—poorly. As poor as it was, it was better than the purest distillation of sadness to come, two hundred proof, in fact, a sadness that exploded rather than poured into me as, shortly after I changed back into my civvies and settled onto the couch, my mother asked, "Will you call your father?"

When the words were spoken, I was ready for them. I had been ready for them for a long time, had rehearsed my response for years. It rang through my head even as my mother asked again, against my silence.

"Will I call my father? No, I will not call my father," I replied. My father. What ironies could wrestle with the pounding, punishing resonances of the words "my father"? Better to meet it head on, standing as tall and stiff as possible. Just as I can't remember a time during which I didn't want to erase and reinvent myself, I cannot remember a time when I wasn't aware that I was a little bastard.

In me the two worlds of my mother and father met and mixed. My mother is college educated, spoke smatterings of French and Spanish and Swahili, and old volumes of Beckett and Sartre and Camus and Brecht collect dust behind the self-help and airport novels on the shelves in her library. She was, at the time of the Gulf War, an executive vice-president for a large mortgage company. My father, by trade a carpet layer, was un- or ill- or oddly employed, depending on which year you talked to him. He had recently lost his house in Duluth to a bank or the IRS, and moved without protest to his Wisconsin cabin.

My mother's mother had been a Marine during World War II, then went on to a successful career in copywriting and editing. Her first husband had hit the beaches at Peleliu and New Britain with the First Marine Division. Her second husband, the grandfather I knew, was commissioned by the Navy and attended Harvard on the GI Bill, eventually receiving his doctorate in economics there. His brother, Donald, would later go crazy in Paris in 1968, the year of my birth. Donald was then a fallen star—former pal of Jason Epstein and Justin O'Brien, Marius Bewley and Clement Greenberg, translator of articles in the *Nouvelle Revue Français;* now a has-been intellectual, a drunk, Catholic, Irishman from Upstate. My grandfather worshipped his older brother. I worshipped them both, carving out a space in my imagination for Manhattan, jazz, abstract expressionists, Kafka, Schumpeter, Trilling; all of which I opposed to my experience of VFW halls, fathers returning from gut-busting manual labor, noisy work in factories, durable-goods sales, Econoline vans and Chevy pickup trucks in small Midwestern towns where no one was good enough and the drunks had bad humors.

I walked back into the library and picked up the phone. My hand trembled as I dialed. My father never had anything to recover, and I was a great loss to him, a further cause of sadness in a life whose course already hewed to the axial lines of sadness.

"What can I do for ya?" a shrill voice answered. My stepmother, who sounded drunk.

"Lonnie?" I asked.

"No shit. Who's this?"

"It's Joel. Remember me?" I asked. "Is my father around?"

"Yeah," she said, startled, then clumsily muffled the phone. I could hear her calling, "Ron! Come 'ere. You'll never guess." She turned her attention back to me. "So what's up?"

"I'm leaving for Saudi Arabia tomorrow morning."

"No shit? They called you up, huh? Some of the kids down at the bar got called up, too. They must be calling everybody up. Hold on." She put her hand back on the phone and warbled the information to my father, who was no doubt remodeling something.

"It's been awhile," he answered nervously, trying to sound together.

"Yes, it has, hasn't it."

"So they called you up, huh?"

"Yes, they did. I'm leaving tomorrow morning for Camp Pendleton. Then to Saudi Arabia."

He paused for a long time, and then spoke with a tremulous hoarseness. "Well, Joel, I have to say that I'm very proud of you . . . I really am. And maybe a little ashamed in front of you. You, the politician and big talker and writer and fraternity man . . . I never really dreamed of those things, but saw them in you even as a kid, in your eyes, always so proud. A proud little shit. When my time came, I just ran away, that's what I do, I run away . . ."

Holding the phone close to my face, I could smell the alcohol, the cigarettes, feel against my skin the thick knuckles of calloused hands curled into a fist, see the lazy eye, slightly bloodshot and squinting, taste the long-familiar bile and hear the silence as he paused, searching for the absolving something to say. What could he? This man of anger and sorrow, sorry catalyst of sad fates, persecutor and victim of wasted youth and wrong living. There are words for this, but they weren't coming. Instead, long, labored breathing, a meditation on his failure in the one good and gracious act of his life, the adoption of a forlorn bastard baby, me. No words, no solace, no comfort, but now broken and hard-labored breathing, the breath of sobs, of SOBS, of drunks, cons, cheats, brawling, wife-and-child-beating sons-of-bitches, liars, fathers. My father.

"Do you have an address so I can write you?"

"No, but I'll call Mom when I get to Pendleton. Mike gave me your address. I've got to be at the airport at six-thirty, and I'm not sure how well the roads are going to hold up. It's snowing like hell down here."

"Here too." He paused again and I could hear the breathing again. "I want you to know," he said, "I want you to know, in case you die or something, that I love you. I do. You don't believe it, but I have to say it, I love you. My eldest, the first and promising son, the bright one who picked himself up . . . Don't be a hero, hey. Don't do anything crazy, all right?" We both paused and then he spoke again, saying simply, "I love you."

The words trailed off into the universe, perhaps being remarked upon by a God who ticked off a lonely check in the plus column of my father's file. He was sobbing freely now, and tears welled up in my own eyes. I began to search for absent words.

I couldn't find them. I still can't. And so, like the old philosopher, I went to war empty-handed.

Combat Duty

WE LEARNED FROM BOOMER that we were going to Saudi Arabia, that we should tell our friends and family that we were going to be serving in a combat zone, that this was real, that "This is the shit, guys," as Boomer said it. "Combat duty. It's your turn now." It was our turn now: thirty-six men and women at last count, and for each of us, it was our turn. Staff Sergeant Grey, "Boomer," was standing in front of our formation. Tall, thick, broken-nosed and slightly stooped from hard living, he was a throwback to John Wayne, to the "Old Corps," the "Hard Corps"—and Vietnam. His uniform hung from him like his skin, well worn and slightly wrinkled. Boomer had served two tours in Vietnam, one as a grunt, slinging a machine gun through jungles and rivers, and another as a truck driver.

On my first day of activation, back in Minneapolis, I had no one to give me a ride to the reserve unit, so I marched two miles to the used bookstore to sell enough books for cab fare. I mumbled something to the clerk about trading books for guns. *Really.* He nodded and handed me seventeen bucks. I also traded my khakis for camouflage trousers, my loafers for combat boots, my wool overcoat for a camouflage parka. Arriving at the unit at 10:30, I approached the ragged ranks of a formation from behind, following the yellow lines painted on the cement floor. I felt like I was sneaking up on more than just the formation.

"Shit," yelled Bergman, "you mean Turnipseed didn't go UA? You aren't gonna send him to war with us, are you, Boomer?"

"Hey, Turnipseed, whatsa matter. No one came to shake your box under the Hennepin Avenue Bridge this morning?" called out Corporal Schuyler.

"Turnipseed," Boomer called, "get your ass in my formation." As it turned out, I was not the only latecomer. It was winter in Minnesota, and farmers had chores or were on vacation, long distances to cover, at any rate. The less nostalgically detained of our group needed to be weaned from a beer and a warm body before standing in our chilled formation.

Staff Sergeant Landers was our other Staff NCO. We weren't sending any officers from our unit, so Landers and Boomer were running the show. Landers had two degrees; Boomer had a Purple Heart and campaign ribbons with stars marking multiple tours.

"Who we missing, Landers?" Boomer asked.

"Looks like we need Schlitz, but he's out in Pipestone, and we need, uh, Sergeant Bernie." Bernie was his *first* name, and in four years together at the reserve unit I never learned his last name. He was a farmer named Bernie. Sergeant Bernie. This was before the Corps started the ridiculous practice of requiring men to sew their names on the front of their camouflage utilities: you should know a Marine's name—or have the dignity or balls to ask for it—before giving him an order (or following one).

After Boomer told us we were going into the Shit, we collected our gas masks. We even tried them on, and then left them on while waiting in line. Heavy, sweaty novelty items. They reeked of fresh rubber, like a new inner tube.

"I'm your father, Luke," Heinemann wheezed obnoxiously to Clem through his round, charcoal-activated mouthpiece. I wasn't sure whether he looked more like Darth Vader or one of Kafka's insects.

"Luke, come to the dark side."

Our faces were still creased with red from the gas mask, like puffy pillow marks, when we collected our ALICE packs.

Inside the packs we stowed our 782 gear: H-harness and magazine pouches for 5.56 mm M-16 rounds, canteens, canteen cup, and canteen pouches, first-aid kit, poncho and poncho liner, shelter half, stakes, and a rope. Nobody knows why the Marine Corps called it 782 gear, but then, being Marines, we called it something else—deuce gear; just like we called hats "covers" and shirts "blouses." All this we stuffed inside our packs alongside a Kevlar helmet and Kevlar flak jacket. We strapped a sleeping bag to the top of our ALICE packs, and a foam rubber pad to the bottom.

"I guess we're 'bout ready for combat duty now, huh?" asked Solter, standing tall with a pack on his back.

"Hey, cheeseball, you forgettin' something?" asked Corporal Joseph.

"What?"

"How the fuck 'bout bullets and a rifle?"

We received our rifles a few days later, at Camp Pendleton. It was already night when we formed up at the armory, the floodlights casting their yellow glow over the cracked tarmac and, our ranks now enclosed within the armory gates, the sagging men standing in wait. Shortly after falling in line and shuffling into alphabetical order, we were told that the armory had run out of rifles.

I walked over to sit against the tire of a semi-trailer parked at the edge of a shadow.

"Hey!" cried a familiar voice. "Hey, Turnipseed—whatcha readin'?"

It was Bergman, the comedian. But no ordinary comedian, for Bergman was a comedian the way Monet was a painter: my moods and outbursts were for his jokes as cathedrals and poplars under the changing light of a coursing sun were for the impressionist's canvases. His uncanny knowledge of my moods caused me fits, and my unthinking reply worked like a new medium for his brush: "Nietzsche."

"Bless you," he said. He paused for the predictable laughs, appreciating his brilliant strokes. "But I was askin' you what you were reading."

Silently, I looked up. "Actually, there is a philosopher named Nietzsche whose works I was just now perusing."

"Yeah? What's *he* say that's so amusing?"

"Would you really like to know?"

"Yeah." "Yeah." "Of *course* we want to know." A small Chorus had formed. "Tell us what philosophy's all about, Mr. Intellectual."

"I suppose it depends upon what sense of 'philosophy' you mean. But then, that was just what I was trying to determine."

"You some kind of snob?" someone asked.

"Isn't that the same thing as philosopher?" asked someone else.

Bergman's eyes rose from their contemplation, as if he'd seen a new quality of light. "Hey, Turnipseed, I got a philosophical question for you: If your brains were gasoline, and you were a piss-ant on a piss-ant's motorcycle, would you have enough gas to go around the inside of a Cheerio?"

"Is it an Apple-Cinnamon, Honey-Nut, or regular Cheerio?" I asked.

Bergman and the Chorus took a smoke break, then returned, hungry—mangy with the ennui of interminable formations and sinister with the desire for mockery.

"HEY, TURNIPSEED!" one of the growing Chorus called from afar. "We decided to ask ya s'more questions about philosophy." They clustered around me.

"Okay," I said as I gathered my book and bag to stand up, "what sort of questions do you have in mind?"

"To start with, why can't you just be, you know, *normal?*"

"He can't be normal, he's *Turnipseed!*"

"Normal? *Here,* I want to be normal?" I paused to catch my breath. "Are you sick? Why am I here, at Armory 13 on Camp Pendleton? To pick up a Colt M-16A2 gas-powered semi-automatic rifle. For what purpose? To kill people. This is normal? Robin, shrieking in the middle of the night, Rosenquist pissing his bed—and we're still in Cali-fucking-fornia—this is *normal?* If this is normal, I'm perfectly happy to be a freak."

Bergman: "And let me be the first to say, 'You're doing a bang-up job.'"

When the laughter died, someone else called out, "See, told you he was going to go all judgmental."

Then another voice—Boomer's—called out, "ALL RIGHT, LET'S FORM IT UP, MINNEAPOLIS!"

The wind had picked up a little, and I was cold and tired as I stood in line waiting for my rifle. After an hour or so, by which time I was so tired I could barely walk, having been marching or standing since dawn or earlier, I received my rifle and left the armory. As I walked through the night, I watched other tired men straggling home in ones, twos, and threes, their backs laden with newly issued gear, their rifles slung lazily over their shoulders: ghosts and shadows of men.

After stopping at the PX to pick up my second, third, and fourth packs of cigarettes—Camel Filters—I headed for my bunk in Squadbay C. I walked alone beneath the smoke-grey skies, sparsely star-shot and faded by the lights of Camp Pendleton. Shadows cast themselves in a dozen directions as I walked past laughing, drunken Marines, past someone pissing in a ditch. Inside the dim barracks, I walked past bunks, some warm with a slumped and snoring body, others crisp, cold, and empty. I undressed by the dull red glow of the EXIT sign, which cast rose shades on my white skin, a whiteness gone pale grey in the light reflected off the well-waxed floors. Silent. And lonely, like a Hopper painting.

Rough cotton sheets cooled my body, wool blankets scratched my bare arms, and the smell of disinfectant clung hard to the sheets, thick and omnipresent, but also comforting. A chill ran through me: the shock of institutional comfort, a saving shock, though severing also, a therapy like electrical shock, separating one's past self from one's present, and marking a surrender to greater forces. The smell of the Marine Corps. Boot camp. Memories of learned response to battle. Memories of a father's ferocity. Of cold stares. Clenched jaws, clenched fists. The ringing metal of Olympic weights slamming down on bench-press arms. The smack of palms against rifles, palms against faces.

Outside, the occasional shouts of drunks rose through night and thought to disturb me as I lay breathing in long, measured rhythms. My thoughts swept quickly, from breath to breath: of Sarah, alone; Mark, with no one to talk to, smoking his pipe quietly in the coffee shop; Dave, fifty miles away in El Toro, doing paperwork late into the night at his chow hall. The shouts outside came closer, like an onrushing wave, and crested with the crashing of boots up the metal staircase.

The fluorescent squadbay lights flickered into brightness. Heads jerked up from their pillows, then yawns and yells competed with a steady succession of ruffling gear, clattering locker doors, rattling buckles and clips, and the razor-sharp chafing of fresh nylon against fresh nylon. I could hear Clem, Heinemann, Solter, Blegen, Corporal Joseph. And Boomer.

"All right, you kids, it's time to get yourselves un-fucked," hollered Boomer, who slept in the bunk below mine. I pressed my face into my pillow, pretending to sleep. The rattle of the lock against the steel cabinet doors, and the rustle of Boomer's rummaging, seemed to originate in my head, like a too-vivid dream. He stood for a moment, breathing the labored breath of a drunk, then kicked his bundle of gear out into the open floor of the squadbay.

"School-circle around me," Boomer called. I rolled over in bed, one eye squinting like a crocodile's, and positioned myself so that I could see, framed between two steel bars, Boomer and his pupils sitting in a circle in the middle of the squadbay; see Solter sitting down after turning out all but one of the fluorescent lights.

Hoarse, with grey-speckled crew cut, Boomer sat at the head of the circle, like a hard-core Mister Rogers. He popped the top of an Old Milwaukee, jerking forward to sip the foam, and put his trademark Winston back into its crook between his lips. *Just like my father.* Rolls of duct tape and white athletic tape sat stacked in the middle of the circle, unsheathed Ka-Bar combat knives rested in laps, or lay on the linoleum, sharpened edges gleaming against the carbon finish of the blades. Scattered in concentric rings were ALICE packs, H-harnesses, E-tools, canteens, flashlights, six-packs of beer.

"Okay, now put your first-aid kit on the back of your cartridge belt,"

said Boomer, holding his own up for inspection, the ash from his cigarette falling, then disintegrating, upon it.

"How're we gonna reach it if it's on our backs?" asked Corporal
Joseph.

"Hey, stupid—listen: if you're gonna need your first-aid kit, *you* ain't
gonna be the one reachin' for it. Your buddy is. Put it in back." Everyone
pulled at the steel clips of their kits, rotating them along the nylon mesh
and steel eyes of their cartridge belts. "All right, now put your canteens
next to your first-aid kits, and your magazine pouches—" he held his
own cartridge belt high again "—right next to 'em, like this." He dropped
his cigarette into his beer can, and began another cycle of beer, cigarette,
and instruction.

"If the shit hits the fan, you wanna have your ammo where you can
get it. You should have a clean strip in front, so you can sit up straight in
your trucks, and lie flat on your bellies, and still get everything you
need."

"Hey, Boomer, when're we gonna get our rounds?" asked Blegen.

"We should get 'em tomorrow. After medical. You'll get 'em before
Saudi, for sure: in case we hit the ground and it's hot."

Corporal Joseph took this possibility with an air of excitement,
draining the last of his beer. "Yeah, I brought my own piece. Think
they'll let me keep it, Boomer?"

"What'd you bring, kiddo?"

"I brought my .45," he replied, cracking another beer.

"Well, you're not billeted as an MP. And you're not a Staff NCO. I *hope*
you get to wear it, but I don't think so. Register that thing with the
gunny whatever happens, 'cause I'd hate to lose your ass to concealed-
weapons charges."

"Don't you think it's funny," asked Blegen, "that they'd bust you for
having an extra weapon when you're at war?"

"Yeah, well, rules bend during war—but not before. *I'm* carrying my
.45 *and* my Beretta. As for that tin piece of shit called an M-16, keep it
carefully—the barrel on that thing'll bend if you fart on it. No shit,

watch over that rifle like it's your sister's baby. Goddam bolt'll seize after you've fired about three rounds, and if it rains you're in a world of hurt. Keep your bolt-cover closed, too: sand will lock that bolt in a heartbeat."

"If the M-16 is such a piece of shit, Boomer, why do they still issue it?" asked Clem.

"Cause *they* don't give a rat's ass about you. That's what *I'm* here for. I'd give every one of your sorry asses an M-14 or an AK if I could find enough of 'em. Course, then you'd have to carry the things." He paused and laughed. "Yeah, you boys gotta take care of each other. The officers and other rear-echelon motherfuckers don't care about you except that they have to feed you and pay for you."

"I thought we were rear-echelon motherfuckers," said Heinemann, dropping his H-harness into his lap.

"Let's get this straight, gentlemen," said Boomer, all seriousness. He took his cigarette out of his mouth. "We're going to be the single most visible target on the battlefield. And there are going to be crashes. Accidents. Casualties."

"Hey, Boomer," said Solter, "where do we put our E-tool? Should we put it on the outside in case we have to dig foxholes? You know, just in case?"

"Put it in the bottom of your ALICE pack," he said, watching Solter wrangle with his gear. "And put your bayonet on the *side* of your cartridge belt so you don't go bending over and stab yourself." Boomer gazed into the distance for a second, his face expressionless. He rotated his cigarette around in a circle with his lips.

"What's ALICE stand for, anyway?" asked Corporal Joseph.

"It's an acronym, dummy," said Solter.

"But what's it *mean?*"

I had been drifting into sleep, but this question was so stupid it woke me up. I called out the answer in a sleep-roughened voice.

"Turnipseed? You awake, kiddo?" asked Boomer. "Why don't you get your butt down here and have a beer with us?"

"Old Mil'!" called Heinemann, "C'mon, Turnip, better drink it before it gets cold."

"*Warm* Old Milwaukee?" I asked. "I'd better get some sleep."

"Shit," he replied, "get real. It's the only beer you're gonna drink for a long time. Besides, we're all in this together now, *philosopher*. Better make the best of what ya got."

Blegen, who had known me since the tenth grade, laughed, "Hell, I bet Turnipseed's got an espresso machine packed in with all his books. We'll be driving by and he'll have a goddam coffee shop set up in a tent on the side of the highway, smokin' his pipe and reading Thoreau. Isn't that right, Turnip?"

"Nietzsche. And a cigarette," I replied. "'Night, guys."

Everyone answered in unison, raising their beers, "'NIGHT, TURNIP!"

Still rolled over with my face in my pillow, I listened as Boomer continued his workshop, initiating the younger men into the realm of forbidden knowledge: soul-rending boredom, fear, the ache of lost love, murder, and death.

Robin started another nightmare—low groans rising from the dark end of the squadbay. A week ago, at our reserve unit in Minneapolis, he startled us by showing up for processing wearing a full H-harness with a shiny new Ka-Bar attached to it. He talked about "kicking some fucking ass," and "getting a goddam field promotion." For a flabby redhead from the sticks, a guy who barely passed his physical fitness tests, and who regularly bore the brunt of comments like "pussy," "fuckhead," and "Hey, Robin, if I ever caught you dating my sister, I'd know she was a lesbian," this appearance struck us as a bit odd. I think it was Bergman who asked him if he was "going to the school play or Saudi-fucking-Arabia." It took two days at Camp Pendleton for his nightmares to start: long, melodramatic affairs that terrified us. As much shit as Robin got during the day, we never fucked with his dreams.

When Robin left REM sleep, silencing his nightmares in pillow-stuffed snores, Solter asked Boomer, "What was it like, Vietnam?"

"Boring." Everyone snickered after Boomer spoke. "No really, I mean it, it was boring. In fact, it's going to get so boring you won't feel like doing anything. Not reading, not sleeping, not shitting, jerking off, nothing."

"War is *boring?*" asked Blegen. "'*Nam* was boring?"

"Ninety-nine percent of the time you just sat around, waiting for the shit to hit the fan. Boredom creeps up on you like a sickness. It makes you stupid."

"Like what?"

"Like you'll start playing with grenades or claymores. Or forget how long it's been since you've written home. That's something else: you gotta write home to your friends, your wife if you got one, and your mother and father. Your family at home is going to mean more to you than anything in the world. A letter from your father will be like a Christmas present. No shit. And that goes both ways: write letters, no matter how tired you are."

"I bet my dad'll write me letters about ice-fishing."

"Yeah, I gotta write *my* dad to find out if we're gonna get that new theater," said Heinemann, whose family ran a small chain of second-run movie houses. "I'll probably manage it if we do."

"I'm more interested in *getting* letters," said Solter, "than writin' 'em. My dad'll send me letters. Wife, too."

"Yeah, my wife's probably baking shit to send me right now," said Joseph.

"That's good. Great. For the rest of you who ain't married, forget about your girlfriend. Just forget her. Remember the smell of her hair, and her pussy, but just forget about her and *expect* a Dear John letter." Boomer's words were repeated as murmurs around the school circle.

I didn't say anything else for the rest of the night. I listened in, now fading, now focused, and felt a form of life slipping away. As if philosophy were not a subject, or a passion, but a way of being, or worse: a pretension. The smell of books was replaced by the smell of disinfectant and beer, gun oil and diesel. The fear of one ignorance traded for another, so that knowing where to put a first-aid kit became more important than knowing Kripke's reading of Wittgenstein; having a father to whom you could write more important than having the Clarendon edition of Locke's *Human Understanding,* in the 721 pages of which *fear* is mentioned once (as "an uneasiness of the Mind, upon the thought of Evil about to befal us"), *love* but once, and *horror* goes unmentioned. Which is what Boomer was for:

"Now, when you *do* see action, you will shit your pants. Or not. I personally was so constipated in 'Nam I shit little brown pebbles I coulda used as ammo. That was, when I wasn't sick with jungle fever and shitting myself, firefight or not.

"Now, the absence of beer is going to be a new element. At least in the Nam you had beer. They'd even airlift the shit out to you. You need to get drunk, shit-faced, flat-out fucked to clear your mind, right? Whose idea was it to have a half-million-man AA meeting instead of a war, anyway?

"You kids *are* gonna see shit that'll tear your heart out. People burned like chicken on the grill, or just an arm, no body, just an arm floating in a puddle. No blood in it anymore, just a white rubbery arm. Like a goddam wax bean, life-sized. And don't take the watch off the damned wrist, either. You gotta just walk by, serious, but not *serious*. Call it a big old wax bean or something, right? Alert, but not lookin' too close." He paused. "It can be tough . . . tough like a motherfucker. You just gotta get through it."

Boomer stopped for a moment to consider his words. "Jesus Christ, I feel like I'm your goddam father."

In Country

OUR C-5 ROLLED TO A STOP at Al Jubayl Naval Air Force Base in Saudi Arabia. There were no lights shining on the highways, or in the city, or even along the runway. I knew before rising from my seat that things were different from what I'd expected; from what I'd thought while lying on a stiff futon a week before; from what I'd thought while sighting a rifle for the first time in years at Camp Pendleton; what I'd thought while staring at CNN and its phosphorescent prophecies in Torrejon; what I'd thought while staring, just an hour before, at a black sky above the fallen lighthouse at Alexandria.

Everything felt strange. Real.

We descended into a world of swirling sands and uncertainties. The floodlights guiding our steps down the ramp cast us in long shadows, like dancing Giacometti soldiers. Boomer called out to us, "Okay, Marines. Hand your barf bags to the airman—we're at war."

"Hey, Boomer, where are we?"

"I told you—we're at war. Anything else is on a need-to-know basis."

And what *did* we need to know? We were Marine reservists, and reservists, I was told by my recruiter, hadn't gone to war since World War II.

"Saudi Arabia, man—no fat chicks."

"What the fuck, Heinemann, you think this is spring break?"

"There's sand, ain't there?"

While the other guys moaned behind me, struggling with their packs and rifles and their civilian selves camouflaged by beige and black and brown uniforms, I wrote KNOW THYSELF on my combat helmet, making a peace symbol out of the O.

We shuffled through a palpable silence, with men moving quickly into formation or driving electric carts from the plane to the buses and five-ton trucks parked nearby. Inside my head, however, there was plenty of noise. I was still back in my seat; back in the Agora of Athens with Glaucon and Socrates: *"A man must take with him into the world below an adamantine trust in truth and right . . ."* Plato was talking to the philosopher who descends from the light of the Ideal into the world of everyday shadows, but standing ankle-deep in drifting sands off the runway at Al Jubayl, at zero-dark-thirty in the morning, five minutes into my first war, it seemed like he was talking to me.

Our ride was a run-down city bus: advertisements in tatters, paint peeling, and all surfaces covered with a thin film of dust and tobacco smoke. It felt like we were driving underwater. The windows took no time fogging, dripping beads of dirty sweat. The sound of men squirming was almost as loud as the dull rumble of the engine.

And then there were the sounds of our commonality, snoring and whispered gossip, which drifted in and out of my consciousness as I drifted in and out of sleep. My half-awake mind took me out beyond the windshield and onto moon-shadowed dunes, out onto the highway, roaming alone and at peace, out through the fantastic, rising refinery towers, intricate and bizarre like long-burned steel candles whose drips have accumulated while flowing down onto the desert, God's drafting table for religions and lunatics. The flames from the burnoff danced and died in a silent ecstasy, only to rise up again somewhere else along the horizon.

When I awoke with a rude jerk, the strange had already become the familiar; war had become work. Our bus was idling at a stop light, just before an overpass, beyond which lay the city of Jubayl. Passing through the dirty, sulfur-lit outskirts, we came up against the Persian Gulf, at night a mere blank horizon whose definition lay in its unbroken blackness. We joined a long queue of trucks, cars, buses, and tankers waiting to pass through the gates. In the far distance, lazy arms passed clipboards, and lazy eyes checked them. In the farther distance, cranes rose hundreds of feet in the air and ship masts blinked warnings to the hovering Hueys and CH-53 cargo helicopters.

We were headed for our first home in Saudi Arabia: Camp Shepard, a tent camp situated on the asphalt wharf at Al Jubayl, the northernmost deep-water port used by the Allied Forces. A quarter-mile into the shadows squatted the city, silent. An MP waved us through the front gate. We drove past the fuel dump, where semi after semi waited its turn to refuel. We drove past the Marine Corps tractor-trailer lot, where hundreds of run-down semis awaited us. Past the Patriot missile batteries, rectangular boxes jutting above camouflage netting, their closed tubes pointed toward the skies. We drove along a four-lane road divided by palms. Just past the heavily protected naval hospital, we passed two machine gun bunkers and turned into the Marine Corps tent camp.

Halogen lights atop fifty-foot poles bathed the entire port in bluish-white: perfectly aligned stars in a drill instructor's heaven. Hundreds of green tents stood in uniform rows on the asphalt grounds of the wharf, which had been abandoned to the Allied Forces: American Army and Navy, American and British Marines, Saudi Arabian Coast Guard, a Norwegian something-or-other, and German water purification specialists. The unsettled, dusty atmosphere felt exactly like, smelled of mildewed canvas, fresh paint fumes, and salt-sweat exactly like, Camp Pendleton or Twenty-Nine Palms. Our bus idled next to the thirty-foot skeleton of an undraped maintenance tent. Bodies buzzed with equal parts expectation and exhaustion, we dragged our load of three seabags, a cot, and rifle per man out into the open asphalt. I struggled with my packs and metaphors, peeking into a dark tent.

"Fuckin' A, Marine. This is an *officers'* tent," someone called through the black.

"This tent's full," someone murmured through the canvas of the neighboring tent.

They had not set up enough tents to house the several busloads of us, and we crept though the camp like homesteading thieves. We weren't much good at thieving, however, since the GP Mediums—the olive drab, sixteen-man tents—were held down in their perfect rows by ropes tied to cement blocks scattered across the wharf. You'd be sneaking along, trying not to wake anyone in the tent whose vacancy you were about to spy, when, from the other side of the tent you'd hear "Jesus—Fuck—Shit—Ow!" then a *thwump* and a clatter: the sounds of a Marine tripping over a rope, smacking his shin on a block, falling backward over another rope, bruising his shoulder blade on the block he landed on, his seabag pummeling the canvas tent, and, finally, his M-16A2 semi-automatic rifle slamming into the deck.

A siren much like a Minnesota tornado warning sounded in the distance, over the roof-tops of the city of Jubayl. Then another siren sounded. The first men started rolling out of the tent flaps, and the tents lit up in quick and random progression, fast, like bursts of contained fireworks. Men wore nothing but boxer shorts, green wool socks, and dangling dog tags. They wore gas masks and splashed through puddles of standing water on their way to a bunker. Any bunker. It sounded as if there were sirens everywhere, and there were: mounted to the same poles in Jubayl that the morning prayer calls rang from, mounted to lightposts above the naval hospital, in the Patriot missile compound, atop the Marine Corps' guard shack, out on the loading docks, up by the British Marines, and at the Saudi Coast Guard station: a deafening canon of defense sirens, like a hundred tornadoes hitting at once. Shit-scaredless men dove into the bunkers, on top of each other, sending the sandbag walls of the bunkers spilling out onto the pavement. The sirens roared, and the sound of scrambling men rose and fell with the waves of warning. I dropped my bags and ran for the nearest bunker, which only stood three feet tall. It was overflowing with men. I looked back at my bags, ran back to them, then to a bunker behind them, itself fast over-flowing. I ran toward it, and as if a film had reversed in mid-showing, men began running out of it, diving out, and there stood a man with a drawn pistol.

Freaked, the man stood in the middle of the melee screaming, "Get the fuck out! Get out! Get out!" He was waiving a Beretta 9 mm pistol, sometimes lowering it and sighting in on the slow-footed. "Get the fuck out, this is an *officers'* bunker." The guy's eyes were as wide as ping-pong balls. "You're wrecking my fucking bunker! Get out! Get out!" He pointed his pistol at dumbfounded men, men with one or two stripes and crossed rifles on their collars: PFCs, lance corporals, and corporals. A sergeant screamed back, "Are you fuckin' crazy?" The gunman looked at him, pointing the 9 mm and wearing the two silver bars of a captain. "This is an *officers'* bunker."

UNITED STATES MARINE CORPS
COMBAT ENGINEER INSTRUCTION COMPANY
MARINE CORPS ENGINEER SCHOOL
PSC BOX 20069
CAMP LEJEUNE, NORTH CAROLINA 28542-0069

MATERIAL THICKNESS, IN INCHES, REQUIRED TO PROTECT AGAINST:

MATERIAL	MORTARS 82-MM	HE SHELLS 122-MM	152-MM	BOMBS 100-lb	1,000-lb
SOLID WALLS					
BRICK MASONRY	4	6	8	8	17
CONCRETE	4	5	6	8	18
CONCRETE, REIN.	3	4	5	7	15
WALLS OF LOOSE MATERIAL BETWEEN BOARDS					
BRICK RUBBLE	9	12	12	18	30
GRAVEL, SMALL STONES	9	12	12	18	30
SANDBAGS, FILLED WITH					
BRICK RUBBLE	10	18	20	20	40
GRAVEL, SMALL STONES, SOIL	10	18	20	20	40
SAND✻	8	16	18	30	40
LOOSE PARAPETS					
CLAY✻	12	20	30	36	–
SAND✻	10	18	24	24	48
SNOW					
TAMPED	60	60	60	–	–
UNTAMPED	60	60	60	–	–

✻ DOUBLE VALUES IF MATERIAL IS SATURATED

NOTE: WHERE NO VALUES ARE GIVEN, MATERIAL IS NOT RECOMMENDED

UNITED STATES MARINE CORPS
PHILOSOPHER INSTRUCTION COMPANY
MARINE CORPS GUARDIAN SCHOOL
PSC BOX 31256
CAMP LEJEUNE, NORTH CAROLINA 28542-1256

TIME SPENT ALONE WITH, IN HOURS, REQUIRED TO RECOVER FROM:

MATERIAL	CHILD ABUSE	DRUNK FATHER	A SHITTY LIFE	AYN RAND
PLATO. ATHENIAN PHILOSOPHER-BRAT, CA 450 BC				
THE APOLOGY	40	60	80	170
PARMENIDES	40	50	80	180
REPUBLIC	30	40	50	–
ST. AUGUSTINE. GOD MADE HIM CHASTE, EVENTUALLY, CA 375 AD				
CONFESSIONS	90	120	120	300
CITY OF GOD	90	120	120	300
KIERKEGAARD. NAME MEANS "GRAVEYARD." TAKE IT FROM THERE, CA 1830 AD				
CONCEPT OF IRONY	100	180	200	400
SICKNESS UNTO DEATH	100	180	200	400
EITHER/OR	80	160	300	400
NIETZSCHE. SISTER WAS A BITCH, HE HAD A SOFT SPOT FOR HORSES, CA 1885 AD				
BEYOND GOOD & EVIL	120	200	300	480
ZARATHUSTRA	–	180	240	–
BOURBON. TWO FINGERS, SPLASH OF WATER, CA 1789 AD				
MAKER'S MARK	–	–	–	$10 \wedge 1000$
KNOB CREEK	–	–	–	$10 \wedge 1000$

NOTE: WHERE NO VALUE IS GIVEN, MATERIAL IS NOT RECOMMENDED.

Yusef

WE SPENT THE ENTIRE NEXT DAY building bunkers. In the morning we built them around our tent area; in the afternoon down at Saudi Motors. The ones we built in the morning were pointless—three-foot-high nuisances best suited to preventing pedestrian travel around the tent camp. Our afternoon attempt devolved into a complete cluster-fuck as we tried to build a reinforced bunker without the reinforcements. One of the Vietnam vets had said, "We don't need no goddam Seabees for this shit. Or a manual." Four hours later we had raw hands, sore shoulders, and a few thousand sandbags stacked in a useless pile outside the staff tent.

Saudi Motors was the name of the motor pool where all the civilian tractor-trailers were parked: Mercedes, mostly—the old, round Kurz-hauber models from the sixties, but also Volvos, Isuzus, and even the odd Kenilworth or Mack, with the Marine Corps–appropriate bulldog hood ornament. Most of these trucks were leased from a family outfit called the Khameini Company. Drivers, too—foreign nationals from the Philippines, Cambodia, Ethiopia, Egypt, and Somalia—to supplement the Corps' trained drivers. The Filipinos were everyone's favorites, walking through the lot wearing nothing but blue jeans, T-shirt, and flip-flops. They decorated their trucks with videotape packages from Bruce Lee and Rambo movies. In addition, the Khameinis ran a convenience store out of a trailer and even had a pickup truck available for special orders from the shops in Jubayl. One of the sons—or brothers, maybe—turned me on to, then started stocking, Dunhill and Rothman's cigarettes, and even managed to keep me supplied with a nice Virginia blend for my pipe, along with pipe cleaners and wood matches. He was a regular minor character from a Bellow novel, complete with a degree in finance from Northwestern and a subscription to the *International Herald Tribune,* which he read while sipping tea from a Styrofoam cup.

That long day was broken only by occasional rain showers, cigarette breaks, and by talk about the explosion—the explosion the rest of the port heard while we were scrambling from a Marine Corps captain gone postal. I didn't hear it over the insanity, the sirens, and the *thump-thump* of the Patriot missiles launched from just outside our tent camp, but the guys down at the port saw a huge flash, and some said their chests throbbed from the shock of the explosion. Our command said nothing happened, but word was that guys in the camps outside town had gone MOPP 4—the highest level of NBC alert. In all, we jumped, crawled, stumbled, and groaned through five SCUD alarms during our first night in Saudi Arabia.

In the Marine Corps, NBC is not a network; it's "nuclear, biological, and chemical." MOPP isn't something you swab the deck with; it's "mission-oriented protective posture." Hence MOPP gear, the stuff you wear when you're being nuked: gas mask, charcoal-lined jacket and pants, rubber boots and gloves. In the Gulf, we were ordered to carry our MOPP gear with us everywhere, even to the shitter, along with our 5.56 mm NATO rounds and the M-16's that fired them, our Kevlar helmets and flak jackets, our H-harnesses, which carried our flashlights, canteens, first-aid kits, the magazines holding our rounds, and our bayonets—Ka-Bar knives, too, if you could find a place to attach the damned thing.

Most of us duct-taped our H-harnesses to our flak jackets, which made it easy to pick up and go. It also allowed us to walk around with the cartridge-belt portion of our harness unbuckled, like John Wayne. No shit. You start wearing forty-five pounds of life protection around with you everywhere and you'll start swaggering, too.

A-driving, or riding as assistant driver—riding shotgun—was what we did in the evenings, after bunker-building. After evening chow, taken dolefully in open-sided tents, upon picnic tables lined with Marines, most dirty, some laughing, all tired and glassy-eyed, we would go back to our tents and wait. Wait for morning, for someone else in the tent to come over and bug us, or for someone from the company office to peek into the dim tent and call out, as happened that first week, "Haddad, Turnipseed, Schuyler, and Schlitz! You guys gotta get your asses down to Saudi Motors to go on a run. You got five minutes till the A-duty leaves with the five-ton."

From within the shadows of the tent the four of us looked up at each other, faces surprised by flashlights. It was only six o'clock, but there were no lights in the tent and it was nearly impossible to stay awake. Outside, I could still see traces of sunset on the horizon. After a cigarette, a piss, and a long cold ride in the back of a five-ton, ass rattling on the wooden troop seat, I was awake.

After the A-duty transport dropped us off at the dingy white trailer just inside the gates to Saudi Motors, we checked in at the dispatch desk. There, in the harsh fluorescent light, a corporal handed us slips of paper with license numbers on them. I looked longingly at a coffee pot, which gurgled pitifully, and gave off the aroma of turpentine. Heaven. I felt for my cigarettes, for my Zippo. *I could pull over somewhere and read Whitman over a coffee and a cigarette.*

"Hey, Turnipseed, quit dreaming, wouldya? We gotta get out on the road."

At any given time there were maybe four or five dozen trucks lined up in the lot. During the daytime, you'd have to walk up and down the rows looking for your truck, hoping it might be one of the Volvos or Isuzus. Most often, however, you'd draw a Mercedes—an ancient green semi that both looked and drove like a battered tank. At night you didn't have much trouble finding it, because your driver was there, waiting with the engine idling and the lights on.

When I found my truck, the driver was sitting patiently behind the wheel. He had a long Ethiopian nose, bright black eyes, and his straight, tobacco-stained teeth were framed by a goatee. His dress was like that of most of the drivers, the Filipinos and Cambodians excepted:

sandals, a long white linen robe over blue jeans, and a checkered head-piece held in place with rope bands. Next to him on the seat lay his gas mask: a skimpy nosecone with a charcoal filter screwed on to the end, like the ones over-zealous home-safety gurus use when painting the guest bedroom.

Our convoy commander, a sergeant from Green Bay, walked by with a flashlight in one hand, and a cup of coffee in the other. A cigarette dangled from his mouth as he called out, "Hey, Turn-Speed, it's gonna be a while so why don'tcha get yourself comfortable." You could hear him say the same thing, like a long-diminishing echo, as he walked down the row to tell the other drivers.

I decided to break the ice with my driver by offering him a cigarette, just like in the movies. We smoked silently, looking straight out the windshield like nervous lovers. What should I say? *Well, looks like it's you and me, goin' off to war together. Brothers in arms. How 'bout that?* That wasn't right.

"You speak English?"

"Just little," he said matter-of-factly.

"What, if I may ask, is your name?"

He raised his shoulders and replied, "Yusef."

"How long you been driving a truck?"

"Eh?"

Making steering motions with my hands, like a little kid, I asked again, "Truck?" I nodded stupidly, "Have you drive truck?"

"Oh, no. Not so much. I never work before war. But I am poor, now I drive five months, make money. For war."

"For the government?"

He laughed, raising his cigarette off to the side. "No, make money for me. For my family."

"Yeah? Where do you live?"

He pointed a finger out the window, "Sixty, maybe seventy kilometers."

"And, how many people live there?"

"Ahhh . . . " he began, delighted, "there is thousand homes."

"That's interesting," I said, "it really is." It was more than interesting, and I lingered in the fact that he said "homes," not "houses," or the more atomic census count of "people." I thought of my own dislocations, then tried not to. I asked, "How many children have you got? You got kids?"

"Yes, yes, yes," he answered, "I have seven childrens. One son, he is at universe-ty. Two sons, they are fighting—" He looked with concern at the rifle propped between my legs, the Ka-Bar strapped to my H-harness.

At this time we were interrupted by one of his buddies, who had stopped by to share tea. They invited me to join them, and soon the three of us were sitting cross-legged on a rug laid out next to our truck. A Bunsen burner heated insanely great tea: a kind of fennel or anise and honey and black tea concoction.

While Yusef and his pal talked, I smoked silently, making calculations on homes and families.

So he had four daughters. He was still nodding his head in approval to something our guest had said, when I chimed in, "I go to the university in America. I study philosophy."

After a long, ruminative look, they smiled.

"Yes, well, uh—you know the sky?" I asked, pointing up through the windshield at the first stars appearing above. "I ask question about them. Or," I said, pointing back and forth between us, "or I ask about the people—how they should talk to each other; how they should live."

Yusef nodded. "You talk to me—and sky. Good." A broad smile stretched across his face as he said this, still nodding with approval. He held out a cigarette.

"No thanks, I've got one," I said, pulling one out and lighting it. His buddy accepted one, then looked at me like I'd taken a shit on his rug.

We fell into a silence that smelled like Ronsonol and smoke.

"You want sky?" asked Yusef, looking up at the grimy semi next to us, and then up the halogen lights obscuring the stars. "Me too."

* * *

After they loaded us down with 155 mm rounds at the port, we were on the road to Mishab, about 125 miles north. We always began our runs in Jubayl, where we picked up supplies from either the port or the Jubayl Naval Airport, a few miles up the road from the city. If you looked at a highway map of Saudi Arabia, you'd see a few two-lane highways running from the city of Jubayl to the refineries and gas-oil separation facilities and the airport, then one four-to-six lane divided highway running north all the way to Kuwait City: that would be the Abu Hadriyah Highway. The drivers at Jubayl drove up the Abu Hadriyah to Mishab, where we would drop our loaded semis and pick up empty ones to drive back. The guys at Mishab would then drive their semis straight west into the middle of the desert on a makeshift four-lane highway bulldozed out of the desert, another hundred fifty miles of pea-gravel and dust, past Kibrit, to Al Khanjar—The Sword. Al Khanjar was the largest ammo dump in Marine Corps history: thirty-eight kilometers of blastwall berm containing 151 separate supply cells covering 768 acres, a five-million-gallon fuel farm, a naval hospital with fourteen operating rooms, and two 5,700-foot dirt airstrips. Everything there, and at all the smaller ammunition supply points, was woven into deep bunkered lanes cut out of the desert like a labyrinth. At Al Khanjar, enough ammunition for two Marine Divisions lay stacked on pallets. Rumor had it that more ammunition was stored at Khanjar than had been fired during World War II.

They called us the "Baghdad Express," making our way up the Abu Hadriyah Highway from Jubayl to Mishab, then Kibrit or other Ammunition Supply Points scattered along the route, sometimes miles off the highway along makeshift roads bulldozed through the desert. The desert was filled with small scrub, just like the high Mojave out near Twenty-Nine Palms, but the Abu Hadriyah was nicer than anything between the Palms and Barstow. Except for the occasional camel or Arabic on the highway signs, we could've been hauling gear on a combined arms exercise in California.

As Yusef's eyes stared unblinking at the miles of Abu Hadriyah rolling beneath the dim scan of our headlights, I grew unsettlingly enthused by the prospect of war. I began not to like Yusef, who was not armed like a warrior. He did not have a hundred-twenty 5.56 mm NATO rounds, twenty each in six magazines, with another sixty in cardboard boxes in his ALICE pack. He didn't even have a pack, or MOPP gear, or a rifle, or entrenching tool. No MRES: his meal was a dead chicken wrapped in a plastic shopping bag in the cargo box welded to the side of the trailer. He didn't have a helmet or a flak jacket. Okay, so he made unbelievable tea and he was funny—"You want sky?"—but tea and comedy can't kill. I wanted to reach over and slap him, but lit a cigarette instead. After a few calming drags, I felt ashamed. I still wanted to slap him, to tell him he didn't belong up here, to make him go home to his family and leave the war to the people trained to fight it.

My ALICE pack was sitting between my legs as we came to a stop in Mishab, about twenty-five miles away from the Iraqi front lines. It had been a five-hour drive. Depending on your cargo—and we were always over-limit—you could make the Jubayl-Mishab run in four to six hours, not including the time it took to take on your load down at the port. Mishab was dead quiet, unlike Jubayl, which had, following the first couple nights of the air campaign, resumed a kind of normalcy. In Jubayl, the prayer call still sounded from the loudspeakers scattered throughout the city, five times a day. But those same speakers also sounded the SCUD alarms for the civilians in the city. In Camp Shepard, you always heard the sirens from Jubayl first, which was confusing, because you'd have to wait a few seconds to determine whether it was the muezzin telling you to point your head toward Mecca, or Civil Defense telling you to point your ass toward a bunker. You also had to wait to see whether a SCUD or MIG was coming downrange or whether someone was just having a bad day at the mayor's office: the civilians did not have accurate radar, or a strong sense of reality, and so cranked the false alarm to the point of distraction. To add to the confusion, the U.S. Army maintained a separate set of radar-guided alarms from the Marine Corps. The British had their own alarms, and so did the German water purification units, the Norwegian medics, and the Saudi Arabian Coast Guard. Sleep was impossible, and going out on convoys was a great way to kill off the night.

Now I could hear the distant grumble of earth beneath shells. I was in the *real war*—or, if that didn't exist, I was closer to enemies with guns. I had tried, on the drive up, to wrap my philosophy around this unsettling fact: even though I felt deep within me that this was a stupid war, an avoidable war, I wanted very badly to see the worst of war. As a would-be philosopher, I knew Pascal's line, "The heart has its reasons which reason does not know," and as a smart-ass I knew Freud's, "The dick has its reasons which reason does not know," but a part of me didn't want to buy the fact that the fist, too, had its reasons.

But another part *did* buy it, and now that I was pissing distance from 500,000 Iraqis, I took my pack with me and stepped lightly out of the rickety Mercedes semi. I strolled confidently toward the dispatch tent to sign off on some papers for Yusef, who sat smoking a cigarette behind the wheel. As I walked across the lot I watched as the distant horizon lit up in shadows and light, like the fireworks one suburb over.

"Them Iraqis are wastin' their shells on an abandoned refinery," said the corporal who greeted me in the office. "FROG missiles or something, I guess. We don't worry about that shit unless our SCUD alarms go off. Them or the FOX chemical detection units."

I asked, "Then what do you—"

I was interrupted by the case in question. The explosion was *behind* us, if it was an explosion—and not a jet breaking the sound barrier or an artillery piece firing nearby—and occurred just as the sirens began to blare. "MOPP 4, MOPP 4!" the corporal screamed, grabbing his gas mask.

After donning and clearing my own gas mask, I looked up to see Yusef raising dust down the road. His red and amber trailer lights made stars in my scratched gas-mask lenses, and my voice resounded with a rubbery echo as I tore out of the office and ran down the road after him, screaming, "Hey! That's *my* fuckin' ammo, you dink! You freak of fucking nature, bring back my fucking truck!"

After about a hundred yards of mad protest, I stopped. Each breath blew half its contents out the side of my gas mask, and my heart shook inside my chest like an engine running on three cylinders.

Coming the other direction down the road from Grand Theft Yusef was a warrant officer in a Hummer, looking pissed.

"Goddammit! Who ordered you to go MOPP 4!?"

Standing stupid and alone at the bare end of the lot, I was the first person he saw. I looked at him through my heavily misted goggles.

"Take off your mask, Marine, there ain't no damned gas around here."

It took me a while to consider. After all, how do you know this guy isn't some nut—he joined the Marines, didn't he? How do you know you can trust a guy who in the face of danger is more than anything proud of the fact that he's brass balls and bullet-proof? He didn't stay to bother with me: my first deep breath after removing my mask was of the diesel exhaust from his Hummer as he accelerated past me.

Nerve Pills

IN DESERT STORM, as in all wars, some things were real, tangible: bombs, deaths, cold showers and stinky socks; other things are more shadowy, suspect: Patriot missile accuracies reported in whole numbers, "military justice," the origin of a pallet of new uniforms sitting next to Corporal Rat's cot. Of course, the most profligate product of this or any war, and the most shadowy, is the rumor. The rumor mill churns out products whose adaptability is the envy of every gene pool. Today's rumor, mutated several times over from the incident at Mishab the night before, was that Haddad and I *shot* at our drivers as they drove away down the highway. Maybe it began as *shouted*. When the alarms went off and shit started exploding and Haddad's driver took off, right behind mine, Haddad didn't even get to shout—he was stuck in the dark taking a crap in a Satellite.

Now, back in Jubayl, back in formation, I rocked back and forth on my heels. The salty air from the Gulf put surreptitious sizzles in our cigarettes, and we groaned in the heat. Only January, and already in the sixties. I looked over at Haddad, and we exchanged looks of self-recrimination: *What, was I* supposed *to shoot the guy?*

"I mean, ten tons of 155 mm rounds is fungible, right?" Haddad whispered.

"I suppose so, but then again, so are we," I replied.

We were reservists. We had a decent vocabulary. But when we arrived back at camp around dawn, me and Haddad, sitting on the laps of Schuyler and Schlitz, without our trucks, or their drivers, we were at a loss for words. "They bolted, man," was as much eloquence as we could muster. So we were shitbirds, half-assed, fucked up—*reservists*. So were half the rest of the people in the Gulf: accountants, programmers, me-chanics, lab techs, engineers, electricians, plumbers, one guy was a state representative; me—a *philosopher*. We weren't cold-blooded killers.

"All right, listen up, everyone," called Staff Sergeant Landers. Lan-ders was a DWI lawyer when he wasn't playing Marine in Saudi Arabia. "Okay now, the squad leaders are going to be handing out some pills. When they're done handing 'em out, I'm going to tell you what to do with 'em."

"Shit-can 'em," someone yelled. Everyone laughed.

"You're *not* gonna shit-can 'em, okay?" said Landers. "I'm gonna give you the instructions when we get 'em passed out. Meantime, I got some word to pass. Seems a couple of you ran into some trouble last night with these foreign nationals we been riding shotgun for."

"TURNIPSEED, HADDAD, TURNIPSEED, HA HA HA." Our names rang out from the formation like freestanding jokes. Haddad flashed me another look, frustrated and lost: *Well, what do you do when you're at war and your driver abandons you up at the front fucking lines? Last week I was designing hard drives, for Christ's sake.*

"Okay, okay, you can laugh all you want later," said Landers, raising his voice, which was high and squeaky and Scandinavian, "but this could happen to any one of you. Okay," he continued, "you are not s'posed to use deadly force on these guys if they run away. The last thing we need here is any kind of *incident*. Everybody understand?"

Nobody understood, but everyone nodded and groaned in assent.

"All right. Everyone got their pills?" asked Landers.

Bergman raised his hand, "Yeah, we got 'em. You want 'em back now?"

"No, now listen. You've got two packets of pills. The little white ones you're s'posed to take once a day. The little oval-shaped yellow one you're supposed to take two of. You got that? White—one, yellow—two. Any questions?"

A century-old Soldier's Tale, as told in books and film—*The Enor-mous Room, All Quiet on the Western Front, Good-Bye to All That,*

Catch-22, M*A*S*H, Apocalypse Now, The Things They Carried, Full Metal Jacket, and *Dispatches*—manifested itself in the first response:

"Pie-roh-dos-dah—fuck it, if I can't *say* it, I ain't eatin' it. Oh no."

In the second response: "Little, yellow, different—but it sure as fuck ain't Nuprin. Turnipseed, you gonna sue the government for us if Landers pussies out?"

In the third: "Hey, it says here, 'Do not take until nerve gas had been confirmed by corpsman or medical officer.' What's up with *that?* We get gassed or something?"

The fourth: "Yeah? What the fuck is this? This ain't no Agent Orange shit, is it?"

Turns out, U.S. and British soldiers later said they "smelled something like ammonia" outside Jubayl on January 19 and 20, the night the crazy captain freaked out on us in that bunker. They stated that a "burning sensation," dizziness, and nausea accompanied these explosions. Some were told by their command that the noise was a sonic boom and their irritation was caused by the exhaust from the jets. Funny that the pills would be distributed so soon after a jet flew overhead.

Years after the Gulf War, I read in a report that on January 23, M8 chemical alarms had gone off at Khafji, just north of Mishab. A Marine Corps staff sergeant stationed there said that his unit was told not to go to MOPP 4. They didn't, and the next day a bunch of his men became sick.

The report also stated that on the same day, chemical alarms went off at an unnamed division supply area about twenty miles from Khafji. Could the "unnamed" area have been near Al Mishab? I looked down at the stack of notes out of which I was reconstructing my war: journal entries on loose scraps of paper, the stuff dredged from uncertain memory. I thought I was at Al Mishab with Yusef on January 24. Could it have been the 23rd? Could I have been exposed to nerve gas? Maybe I was misled by the blustering warrant officer in the Hummer who told me not to go MOPP 4.

Any good noncommissioned officer will tell you that uncertainty is the biggest cause of fear among his troops, that, like Plato's guardians, he sometimes *has* to lie to quell uncertainty. I suppose that helps explain why the Gulf War was the first war whose participants became more afraid *after* the fighting than before: while reading the *New York Times* and surfing the Web in our separate solitudes, we no longer have a sergeant telling us that our six years' nausea is being caused by exhaust from low-flying jets.

I now know that one of the pills we were ordered to take was pyridostigmine bromide. Known to doctors as Mestinon, it is FDA–approved for a single use: treatment for myasthenia gravis, a neurological disorder that blocks the chemical signals the muscles need to function. Its known side effects read like a list of Gulf War Syndrome symptoms: confusion, irritability, tremors, rashes, muscle weakness, memory loss, incontinence, and vomiting. In the face of Saddam Hussein's chemical-weapons threats, the FDA granted the Department of Defense unrestricted permission to use PB as a prophylactic against nerve-gas attacks. But the DOD promised to convey oral and written warnings of its risks to the soldiers taking the pills. It abysmally failed to keep its word.

The Defense Department had little data on the side effects of the pills, but some minimal research had indicated high rates of debilitating side effects. A 1994 U.S. Senate hearing on Gulf War Syndrome determined that the Department of Defense's use of pyridostigmine bromide, with complete disregard for informed consent and despite little research, broke the Nuremberg laws, the Helsinki Accords, and the U.S. Common Rule regarding the use of experimental drugs by federal agencies. This disregard for soldiers' welfare did not occur in a vacuum. Indeed, the nature and number of past violations make the dark, paranoid humor of *Dr. Strangelove* seem less like parody than documentary. In the 1940s, more than 60,000 servicemen were secretly exposed to mustard gas and Lewisite. In the fifties and sixties, the Dugway Proving Grounds and surrounding area were repeatedly used for biological- and chemical-weapons research. Throughout the cold war the "Atomic Veterans" were exposed to radiation—at such now-infamous places as Bikini atoll. During the Green Run test in December 1949, fallout was released over the civilian population of Hanford, Washington. In the covert operation MKULTRA, which ran between 1953 and 1964, the CIA and U.S. armed forces gave huge doses of LSD to servicemen.

War wouldn't be war if something wasn't FUBAR—Fucked Up Beyond All Recognition. This is true of all wars, even such seemingly good and benign ones as the Gulf War. Or World War II. I know this because, in the years after the Gulf War, I've spent countless hours reading Senate hearing reports on it. I've come to recognize that our adulation of the stiff-lipped hero is not only wrong-headed, it is false. Even the Good War was not that good for those who *fought* in it. Nearly a million World War II veterans suffered severe psychological injury, as many as were killed and wounded. That's one in fifty male members of the postwar workforce—one in every office. No wonder they wore grey suits. No wonder my mother's father was a quiet, angry drunk. In the United States, some claim that there are more homeless Vietnam veterans than there are names on the black wall of the memorial in Washington, D.C., and as many Vietnam veterans may have committed suicide in the United States as died in southeast Asia. It wouldn't surprise me. If Gulf War Syndrome turns out to be something less sinister than a plot, but more deadly than a rumor, that would be a SNAFU—Situation Normal, All Fucked Up. Of course, no one wants to hear these things, and this makes the Soldier's Tale a difficult one to tell, even when peppered with funny acronyms.

Back in formation, Bergman's response was the most brilliant: "If you wanted to stick it in our ass, why didn't you make it a suppository?"

To say that he looked put-upon would not do justice to the plaint and despair on Landers's face. After a long, twitchy silence, he sighed, like an attorney trying to coach or bully a stupid client.

"Take 'em. Just take the damn pills, Marines. And after you take them, you're going to go to the company office and sign up for anthrax shots. Most of you should get 'em this afternoon. Furthermore, if you *don't* take the pills, and you *don't* get the shots, your spouses, dependents and beneficiaries may become INELIGIBLE for your SGLI, which is a hundred grand now that we're at war. Just take the pills, Marines. Just take the pills and get the shots. When you need to know the why's and what-for's, the word will be passed."

No life insurance? No way. Still, everyone was silent. The crinkle of the blister packs in which the pills were distributed played a quiet accompaniment of anguish. I turned to Blegen, standing next to me holding the blister pack close to his face, trying to read the fine print. "What, Blegen, like anyone's actually going to take these things?"

"No shit, ain't no way I'm takin' 'em." He paused for a second, grimacing, "Still, I think I better get the anthrax shot. My uncle's a farmer. He gets 'em." He paused again, "I think he gets 'em."

Cigarette

THE NEXT EVENING I went on another run as assistant driver on a convoy. I did not get my anthrax shot; I did not take my little pills. I *thought* about taking the pills, though, which I at least carried with me in my ALICE pack. I bounced along in the back of the five-ton winding its way toward the motor pool, wondering how close or how far I would be to the Iraqis and their nerve gas and SCUD and FROG missiles . . . how close or how far from regretting my ignorance of the little pills, the anthrax shot.

Once assigned, we sat in our trucks, waiting. Lowering my eyes from the dusk-lit dust on the windshield, I looked down at my watch. Stopped. Both hands pointed toward the 11, making 10:55, which would have been bunker-building time. Yesterday. Even my watch was mocking me: I was spending my days building bunkers, and my nights riding shotgun for goofballs and chickenshits.

Sitting beside me on the cracked bench seat of another old Mercedes was my driver. He was hanging his head and one arm out the window, negotiating with fast words and faster fingers—jittery shaking gestures, of what? Desire. The man standing before him, some friend or waylaid bystander wearing the full-blown robe and headband bit, shrugged and held out an open palm, offering a crushed and empty box of Marlboros.

Now that my watch was broken, even time was kept in Cigarette. It was one cigarette and half past a craving when my driver looked at me, eyes heavy-lidded.

"Hey," I said, holding an open pack of Camels, "you want a cigarette?" He smiled. It was not an encouraging smile.

"Would you like a *cigarette?*" No answer. "Oh, you don't speak English?"

I pulled two cigarettes from the box, taking one between my lips, offering the other to him. The flame from my lighter flickered in the wind. His hair was long and wiry, his teeth slightly yellowed. Short whiskers grew around the lower edges of his lips and beneath his chin.

"You want a cigarette, or what?" I said, pushing the cigarette toward him. He took the thing offhandedly, then pointed at an opened package of gum lying in the ashtray. The wrappers were faded Pepto-Bismol pink and covered with dust.

"Oh," I groaned. "No, no thanks."

He smiled again, and gestured with little waves from the gum to me. "No, really, no thanks."

I wondered if he knew more about what happened to Yusef, or to Haddad's driver, than I had. We had heard that the foreign nationals who fucked up, chickened out, or otherwise caused logistical problems for the First Marine Expeditionary Force got worked over by Khameini Company thugs. We had also heard they would all be replaced by more reservists coming in from the States.

The whole affair was confusing as hell. It had to be worse for guys like Yusef and this new guy. Having given up on his proffers of gum and goodwill, he leaned back against his door, smiling warily.

"So you speak no English?" I asked him. "You got a name? What's your mother call you?" I sounded like a bully, even to myself.

He just smiled and held out his cigarette, which already had a long ash dangling from the end. The ash fell in a disintegrating tumble as he raised it.

"Cigarette? It's your name, too, huh? Fair enough. Well, Cigarette, what do you say we get this show on the road?"

I looked up at the steel and gunmetal sky and, leaning forward in my seat, stretched my gaze right up to where the horizon curved north toward Mishab, toward the expectation of more shells exploding in the distance.

"Well, Cigarette, hope you hold up better than your buddy, Yusef. You hear about him? No? Well, he pulled a Shit-and-Split on me yesterday, leaving me stranded and swearing at his departing taillights."

If he *had* heard about Yusef, he had every reason to remain silent: when Yusef returned his truck, still laden with ammunition, he got the shit kicked out of him by the Saudi contractors responsible for him. Or was it the Saudi cops? The rumor mill was never very clear about these things. We had no doubt that the drivers who'd abandoned their missions had gotten the shit kicked out of them, though. No doubt about it.

Under a cloudy sky, our convoy arrived at the airport for loading. Helicopters—Hueys, Cobras, some CH-53's—were aligned neatly row after dark row, hunched, blades sagging, behind the hurricane fence running from the boarded-up terminal to the gates at which we waited. In the distance I could hear the grumble of forklifts and the low whine of a cargo plane. The only illumination came from floodlights aimed at the loading area, where an occasional cloud of dust rose above the pallets.

Three cigarettes later the truck ahead of us pulled forward through the gates, unsignalled and abruptly. Cigarette jerked forward in turn.

"STOP, STOP, STOP, GODDAMMIT!" Out from a thunderous, floodlit whirlwind of dust and profanities came a master gunnery sergeant. Cigarette slammed the brakes with a deafening squeal. I raised my forearm, batting down the boonie cover and the wrinkled, greying head flying into my passenger-side window.

"JEEZUS FUCKIN' H. CHRIST! DID ANYONE TELL YOU TO PULL FORWARD?" he screamed.

Did this man know that my driver was not only named, but only spoke, Cigarette? He greeted the master gunnery sergeant with the same shrug with which he first met me.

"SO YOU DON'T SPEAK THE DAMNED MOTHER TONGUE, HUH?" yelled the master gunnery sergeant.

He looked to me.

"So he don't speak the language. You speak the language, Marine? Sure you do. Don't let him go nowhere until he's ordered to, got that?"

He was now standing on the running boards, leathery face stuck into the cab, and I wondered whether I should knock him back asswards onto the sand with the butt of my rifle.

"Well—" I began.

"That's right. Now you don't let him move a goddam inch till I say 'go.'"

My shoulder twitched in hesitation, just long enough for him to hop down and shuffle away, bow-legged and wobbly with anger. As he passed back into the magical clouds of lighted dust, he continued screaming, "GODDAM FOR'NERS! CAIN'T WORK FER SHIT, CAIN'T TALK FER SHIT, AIN'T WORTH A SHIT. HOW THE HELL'S A MAN S'POSED TO GET ANY-GODDAM-THING DONE. GODDAM CORPS'S GONE TO SHIT, WAR'S GONE TO SHIT, DON'T EVEN SHOOT REAL BULLETS ANYMORE . . . GOTTA FLY FAKE GODDAM BULLETS TO BUMFUCK, EGYPT. GODDAM . . ."

By way of apology, I turned to Cigarette and spoke my condolences: *Camel Filters*. Cigarette nodded silently. *Zippo, my friend*.

We were asked to pull ahead by a PFC wearing Day-Glo flightline ear-protectors and greasy overalls. He just appeared around a corner, all of a sudden, waving bright red cones. Then he disappeared.

No smoking was allowed inside the airport compound. *No smoking*. I just stared at the window as one by one the raindrops erased the dust. It had rained nearly every day we'd been in country. The rain rinsed dark streaks down the sides of 155 mm rounds piled on pallets stacked higher than a man's head. After a while, I passed through to the other side of boredom, and began noticing the faint sparkles in the windshield, how the rain pitted the sand along the edges of the ammunition-laden pallets. Corporal Schuyler came by for a minute, walking past with his hands in his pockets. He looked up at me. "Just bored as all fuck," he said.

A forklift rolled by with a load of—*kegs?* I jumped down out of the cab, and into the drizzle. Shivering, I walked around to the bed of my trailer, which had already been loaded with several pallets. Another forklift came by. I flagged it down.

"Hey!" I hollered, "What's in the kegs? Beer?"

"No," the driver answered, "just napalm." He looked so matter-of-fact. "For putting out the fires, and clearing the foliage. You know, the *ground* attacks."

"Foliage?"

Cigarette was strapping down the last of the pallets, squinting at me in the light rain. The forklift operator turned around and bounced off into the floodlights as Cigarette slammed the trailer storage box shut.

I had no idea when I'd fallen asleep, but I awoke with a jolt. And then another. Our truck felt like it was flying through Oklahoma turbulence. I tried gaining my bearings, but couldn't see beyond the edge of the road. There was no moon, no stars, no shadows. No discernible shapes, and the road ahead was barely visible under the dim running lights we used near the front lines. Cigarette was listening to staticky Islamic yodeling on the radio. *Prayers*. The amber glow of the dash lit up the windows, so that all I could see was my own reflection, like an old film negative. I looked over at Cigarette and began to worry.

"Hey, slow down, man."

His eyes were bloodshot and wide open, and he held the steering wheel tightly. I turned around to see if we still had our load. We had our load, but I couldn't see any truck lights behind us. Or ahead of us. We were driving one of the hastily engineered dirt roads connecting the Abu Hadriyah Highway to the ammunition supply points, or ASPs. They were basically made of gravel dumped in the desert and then driven over by tanks. Compared to the civil engineering marvel of the Abu Hadriyah, these things were a goddam nightmare. It was hard to believe we could even drive them. We hit another bump and I flew up, almost smacking my helmet against the ceiling.

"Hey, slow the fuck down."

Of course, he only spoke *Cigarette*. The speedometer was broken, but the RPM gauge read close to 3000, which on an old diesel is redline. *Way past redline.* Cigarette's hair stood out in scraggles, like barbed wire, and his lips curled in a grimace.

"Okay, cut the crap!" I screamed, reaching over to lift his leg with my arm. He swatted at me as we hit another bump, which threw me back against the passenger door. I held my head low and closed my eyes, trying to take deep breaths. *"Okay, don't do anything stupid. Napalm doesn't just explode when it hits the road. He knows what he's doing. You're not actually inside Iraqi territory. You're a Marine, trained to face this kind of pressure. Calm. Collected——"*

We hit another bump, a big-ass, frame-rattling, helmet-tossing crash. When the Mercedes settled back onto its suspension again, I grabbed my M-16, swinging it with my entire body, slamming my back against the passenger-side door.

"LISTEN, YOU STUPID SONOFABITCH, STOP THE FUCKIN' TRUCK."

Cigarette turned slowly and looked at me: barren, lifeless. The prayers on the radio continued to fill our cab. I pulled the charging handle back on my rifle, sending a round into the chamber: clack—click.

He stared straight ahead. He slowed down. Evidently my rifle spoke Cigarette, too. The whine of the engine fell to a soft whisper. I rolled down the window, calmed by the cool mist. I closed my eyes, but I didn't dare dream.

Nerve Pills Redux

HAD THE MARINE CORPS been responsible for Genesis, it would have gone something like this:

"In the beginning was the Word, and it was passed.

"And then it passed that it had changed.

"With the dawning of the third day, it changed back.

"Then, unsatisfied with the creation, it became something completely different.

"The fifth day remains 'Classified.'

"The sixth day is listed as 'Missing.'

"On the seventh day, having completed nothing, they said, 'Fuck it, drive on.'"

We watched Staff Sergeant Landers through dry, stinging eyes. The Navy Corpsmen responsible for our health were standing at his side, whispering into each other's ears. I hadn't gotten back from Mishab until four that morning. I hadn't sagged onto my cot until five.

Now it was six-thirty, and the grey tinge of the world, a grey upon grey, and black, and olive drab, a grey upon the brown and beige of our chocolate-chip uniforms, came no more from the atmosphere or the earth than it did from my own mind. I tried to pay attention, but drifted in and out of sleep as I stood in the morning haze.

"Okay, Minneapolis," droned Landers, "I got some new word on these pills we've been takin.'"

"What pills?" asked Bergman. "You mean the ones we shit-canned?"

"Well, for those of you who *followed orders* and *took the pills,*" Landers replied, "I got some new word. I guess a few guys have been experiencing side effects. So stop taking them."

Bergman laughed. "So Robin and all the other dorks who took the pills, like, everyone that took them had side effects? Yeah, give me some of *those*. Shit, not even Turnipseed was stupid enough to take 'em."

"Yeah, this some kind of Agent Orange thing going on here?" asked someone else.

The Navy Corpsmen looked prune-faced, like they were busted, but not about to tell anyone the details.

"Listen," said Landers, "they're just pills, that's all. You can have side effects . . . what did you expect?"

"I expected the big, green weenie," Bergman replied. "That's why I didn't take 'em."

"Yeah, I mean, why we gotta take something that's gonna fuck us up if there ain't no nerve gas?"

"You never know, Marines," Landers said. "You gotta take what they tell you to, because you never know what's gonna happen."

I still don't know what happened. I just know that whenever I have a headache . . . or my kidneys hurt . . . or I run out of breath on a short jog . . . or can't sleep or don't feel hungry or can't concentrate or am irritable . . . or forget something . . . I wonder whether I should or shouldn't have taken the pills; whether I should or shouldn't have worn my gas mask in the bunkers; whether I should or shouldn't have kept my own records of the shots I received at Camp Pendleton.

Friendly Fire

EVEN WITH THE CHAOS of our A-driving missions, these early days had only a provisionally martial quality about them: we were at war, certainly, but for the most part we tried to maintain a kind of civility. We woke up in the morning, stood in formation, trucked down to Saudi Motors, bought Kentucky Fried Chicken from the back of a Khameini Company pickup truck, and watched movies at night in the outdoor theater. At Camp Shepard, the war was more like an interruption of the movie: when the sirens sounded during *Heartbreak Ridge*, the projectionist would stop the film and dive for a bunker, sure: but he was the first guy out of the bunker at the all-clear, and the film was rolling before you could snatch your ass back to the bleachers.

On January 29, the Iraqis upped the ante by crossing the border into Saudi Arabia. They came in all along the border with the First Marine Expeditionary Force, most significantly about fifteen kilometers from Al Khafji, which was a camel spit from Al Mishab in "fourth-largest army in the world is invading" terms. By midnight, two Iraqi armored brigades owned the city of Al Khafji, which had largely been abandoned to a Marine Recon and SigInt post and a few Saudi reservists. With heavy artillery and air support from the Marines, and air strikes from the U.S. Navy and Air Force, Saudi and Qatari forces took Al Khafji back in two days. The Iraqis lost thirty-three tanks, twenty-nine armored personnel carriers, and 137 POWs.

The Marines lost twelve men during the action at Al Khafji—all to friendly fire. In the first incident, a guy accidentally fired a TOW missile into his buddies' Hummer. Four Marines died. About an hour later, an

Air Force A-10 fired an infrared Maverick missile into the back of a Marine Corps Light Armored Vehicle, killing seven. Six days earlier, two Air Force A-10's—aiming for an Iraqi truck in southern Kuwait—had strafed a couple of Marine Corps Recon units south of the border, killing one Marine.

We learned about Al Khafji in snatches, from guys getting back from runs or reports on Armed Forces Radio and Television Service. I learned about it on my way home from Saudi Motors. I stopped by the post office, a Conex railcar box, to pick up my first piece of mail in Saudi Arabia: the *New Republic*, which my grandparents got me as a gift. The cover showed Beethoven wearing a Mohawk and an earring.

Solter came into our tent and immediately railed on me, "You pick up anyone else's mail?"

"No."

"How come you're so selfish all the time? I mean, how come you can't just be nice?"

"Why can't you just let me read?"

I liked Solter. I didn't really have anything personal against anyone. It was the aggregate that was driving me apeshit. I wanted to be back in a coffee shop reading Wittgenstein. Instead I was always being asked to give an opinion on the state of 9 mm pistols or Motor Trend's Car of the Year.

"We let you read all you want," said Solter. "It just, you know, we're a band of brothers, right? Anyway, I just came to tell you you're getting put on guard duty tomorrow. You gotta move out."

"Turnipseed's moving out?" yelled Bergman. "Thank fucking God."

God. God I learned about at the heel of a size-five Ked sneaker. I had been baptized Catholic as a baby, and that was about the extent of my religious experience until fourth grade, when I was living in Little Chute, Wisconsin. My childhood exposure to religion was limited to the expressions "goddammit" and "jesusfuckingchrist." One afternoon, while walking home from school, some of the nicer children in the neighborhood asked me, "Hey, Turnspeed, what church do you go to?"

"Church?"

"Yeah, church—you don't go to church?"

"Nope."

"Don't you believe in God?"

"God?"

This was a foreign concept to me, like asking a nine-year-old whether he believed in the circumnavigation of the globe by medieval Chinese naval expeditions: why, after all, would I believe in a swear word? Strangely, this innocent question—and my seemingly straightforward answer—left me pinned down by two of the kids while the third punched me silly. And so I first learned about God and the ways of His children.

Two hours after my spat with Solter, just as the projector was beginning to roll the coin toss of the best Super Bowl in a decade, I found myself sitting in the chapel. I had a dull sat-too-long ache and an exuberance with a short half-life, like an emotional photo-negative of vertigo, like I wasn't afraid to do something, but should have been. I was exhausted and didn't know what to do with myself.

The chapel was not a church, but a GP Medium, like the rest of the tents—a supply tent cleared out for an hour or two of peace. The chaplain was bald, with a splotchy face. His entire appearance, from unpressed Navy uniform to badly trimmed mustache, combined with his awkward manner, made him seem misplaced, out-of-sorts. The pews were not pews, but two semi-circles of folding metal chairs. Upon them sat men in olive-drab T-shirts and maroon running shorts, others whose camouflage blouses were caked with salt and dust, others freshly showered with spit-shined boots and creases running up their shins. The chaplain read a scene from Acts, where Paul is headed back for Jerusalem, and tarries a while in Syria. All his sackcloth-and-ashes buddies are begging him not to go. Instead they find disciples and tarry seven days. Then Paul leaves for Jerusalem, unafraid. The chaplain turned this into a lesson: "All we need to do is tarry seven days and we can face the task of war undaunted, protected by the Lord."

Why he chose "tarry" to mean "pray" I have no idea, because even Paul said they had prayed. Frustrated, I corrected him.

"'Tarry' means 'wait'—not 'pray,'" I said.

"Hey, dude," said one of the other Marines, "this is the chaplain speaking. He's got a college degree."

I laughed.

"So you are suggesting that 'tarry' means 'wait'?" asked the chaplain.

"Yeah, you know, like 'Don't tarry, now.' What, like your grandparents were telling you not to *pray?*"

"I'm gonna have to say I'm with the chaplain on this one," someone said.

"Yeah, chaplain's right."

"Listen," I said, "these guys prayed on the beach. We can still have the lesson, but 'tarry' means 'wait.'"

"Perhaps it does mean 'wait,'" said the chaplain, "but do you Marines agree that the lesson would still be preserved?"

"Yeah, the Lord is the shit," one of them said, "You stick by him, he'll carry you through."

I didn't even listen to the rest of the sermon. I tried instead to make something of the metaphysical difference between 'tarry' and 'pray.' I knew the score of the Super Bowl, because I had already paid out to Blegen. I should have watched the game anyway.

When the service was over, I stayed to fold the tablecloths in a sort of quiet penitence. It was just me and the chaplain and this guy wearing shower shoes whose chin did not yet sprout hairs and whose nose looked like a stone axe.

"You're a pretty sharp young Marine there, Marine," said the chaplain.

"Yeah? I study a lot of philosophy."

He spent a good fifteen minutes doing the tiresome "love" thing with me, *agape*, and *philia*, and *eros*, and whatever the other one is, as if the Fowler brothers took a break from their eternal submissions to the *Oxford English Dictionary* to simultaneously possess him for a quick earthly quarrel. He was interrupted when our third broke in with, "I just know I *love* Jesus, no matter how many Geek words there are for it."

The chaplain and I looked at him.

"And your name is?"

"Salerno. I'm from Texas."

"It's a pleasure to meet you, Salerno. How did you enjoy the service?"

"It was pretty good till ol' Turnipseed ruined it with all that philosophy stuff. I couldn't understand a word he said, even the ones I knew."

"Yes, well, he did change the tenor of the conversation, didn't he?"

"How come you messed it up like that, huh, Turnipseed?"

"Because I want to get to the bottom of shams and hypocrisy, unlike the Marines, unlike the guys watching the Super Bowl over there in the theater."

"But the truth is simple, right?" asked Salerno.

"The Lord is Truth," intoned the chaplain. "And the Lord is, though simple, a mystery whose answer we seek in prayer and in chapel. In that respect, it was a valuable service that Turnipseed provided. I'm curious, though—why do you use 'Marines' in the third person? Aren't *you* a Marine, Turnipseed?"

I stood naked in my disgust, and tried quickly to cover myself with a fig leaf of dissimulation.

"It's a sort of philosophical obliquity thing. I mean, I often think of myself in the third person. You know, always looking for the Archimedean point."

Which, though true, didn't satisfy either of us, though we let it drop with the last of the folded table cloths, stacked candles, crosses, hymn books and little camouflage-covered bibles: Gideons in fatigues. Outside, Salerno continued to grill me on faith and reason.

"You don't believe in God, or what?" he asked.

"No, I can't say that I believe in God, Salerno."

"Well, *what're you doing here?*"

"I believe in peace and quiet and a sort of thoughtfulness about things—*here* is the only place I could find it."

He laughed, and then, abruptly, paused. A look of struggling profundity came over him, as if enlightenment were almost but not quite breaking through the heavy clouds of his consciousness, as if Strauss's *Zarathustra* was playing and a little sprout of thought was time-lapsing its way to daylight. "It's kinda funny, isn't it, though," he began, pausing again, this time to raise his chin and tilt his head. "It's kinda funny that you're so smart about a little truth like a Geek word, or a philosophy stuff, but that you don't see the real big truth, like the only truth there is and that's Jesus. That's right—Jesus! Jesus right here in Camp Shepard."

"Right here in Camp Shepard?" I asked with a lilt, half expecting a Broadway production of *The Music Man* to pop full-blown out of nowhere.

"And I'm here to tell you about it. Jesus that is, who is a *Him* not an *It*, but who loves you right here where you're standing and you'll just have to 'fess up to it, Turnipseed."

"Let me just throw something out here, Salerno. Have you ever heard the phrase 'bearing the cross'?"

He stood there grinning for a minute, like he was trying to compose himself at the Academy Awards or something, "It's a light load, ain't it?"

"No," I said, "It's a heavy load and it's uphill and people spit on you and you have these thorns digging into your skull and blood and sweat dripping in your eyes, and all this struggle is so you can carry yourself up to your death, to the scene where your father will forsake you. What the fuck, are you some kind of nut you don't know this?"

"I'm some kind of nut for Jesus, brother."

I could do nothing but watch as he turned back toward the tents in which we lived, on whose sides the blue glow of the Super Bowl still flickered in reflection. Off he went, alone and cheerful—a scowling cheer, a Savanarola in shower shoes, flip-flopping his way to a respectable head-count in saved souls.

Overhead, helicopters began circling. The naval hospital compound was divided from our tent camp by a black plastic–sheathed hurricane fence, rising twelve or fourteen feet and topped with rolled concertina wire. As the helicopters began landing on the other side, hovering over the silvery Tyvek-wrapped surgical tents and interconnected maze of olive drab GPS, I began walking quickly. The battle of Khafji was on. This could be the shit, the real actual war and not semantics and A-driving for dazed Ethiopians or building bunkers or diving into them during false SCUD alarms. I clambered up the sandbag wall of a plywood and four-by-four bunker. Clusters of Navy Corpsmen were huddling near the helipads. I could just barely see their heads over the fence. One of the Hueys had landed, and the corpsmen were unloading something: body bags. Had to be. But I couldn't see anything but heads moving around. I imagined the bags, slick black rubber in the drizzle, reflecting the omnipresent halogen haze of the wharf.

I stood watching the corpsmen's heads until their black baggage was scuttled into the Navy's dark network of tents. I stood watching until the helicopters lifted from their pads and out over the Gulf. Then the compound became quiet again, the asphalt a vast expanse of empty, shimmering grey.

Guard Duty

"REACT, REACT, REACT!"
The words crashed through my dream.

"React, react, react!"

Sergeant Small strode through the tent, smashing our cot frames with a nightstick. In the dark, men began to roll out of their cots, grabbing their rifles and gas masks. There were no SCUD alarms, but guys began moving as if there were. The light clinked on, and Todd sat on the edge of his cot.

"React to what, exactly?" he asked.

"Get on your gear, third shift, get on your gear and get out on the truck. We got a live round up at Post Four. React, react, react!"

We bailed out of the tent in full gear. A five-ton was waiting outside. Sergeant Small pulled me aside.

"Turnipseed, you're on radio."

Beside him sat an old PRC-47 field radio, left over from Vietnam. Thing probably weighed twenty pounds. Riding at the top of my pack, antenna rising high above my head, it made me feel like a Weeble as I climbed into the five-ton. Sergeant Small gave the order to lock and load before we drove out past the machine gun bunker at the entrance to the tent camp. It was two-thirty in the morning, and a light fog hung over the port.

This was guard duty. And the REACT patrol was a pointless exercise within a pointless exercise: go to bed wearing boots and camouflage, then jump out at zero-dark-thirty to run around the camp responding to a fake emergency. That's right—there was no live round at Post Four.

Only a mildly depressed and deeply bored supply clerk serving his month on guard duty. Pointless? The entirety of Camp Shepard, which we were guarding, was already buffered by the port area, which was walled within barbed-wire fence rising twenty feet out of the desert. Not to mention that it bustled with the constant activity of tens of thousands of well-armed Marines and Army soldiers, as well as British Marines, Saudi Coast Guard, and all the other rifle- or submachine-gun-toting assholes who appeared out of nowhere to stand in front of me whenever I tried to get a cheeseburger at the fast-food trailer outside the tent camp. Todd lived in the cot next to mine. Small, the sergeant of the guard, wore tinted Polaroid sunglasses and was a hundred-and-thirty-five pound highway patrolman from South Carolina. He wore a pencil mustache and had freckles.

Heinemann, the only other guy from Minneapolis to pull guard duty, was posted to the interior guard. The interior guard spent their days at a bunkered machine-gun nest at the entrance to our tent camp. I was posted to the exterior guard, the rotation of men who guarded the entire port area of Jubayl. Guard duty seemed, for about the first half-hour, like a good thing: tents with well-built wooden frames, "hardbacks," which also meant smooth wood floors, lights and switches, in a word, "comfort." In four, "good-bye to all that." A fresh start. Even though it was only a few hundred feet from the Minneapolis guys and the Sixth Motor Transport Battalion tents, the distance was measured in routine and hierarchy: different routines and different hierarchies dividing me and the remainder of the men from Minneapolis into separate worlds.

And then there was formation. Not the formation I had grown accustomed to at weekend reserve drills, where it was taken for granted that although I would be late and rumpled, I was at least good for formation, and even for taking the cracked transfer case out of the five-ton that Rosenquist had backed up under load in high gear. No, this was

Sergeant Small's formation. I noted, as I stood back in the third rank, that he was asking people to perform a rifle manual, or drill, Inspection Arms, which I had not practiced in the four and a half years since I'd graduated from boot camp. He and the Corporal of the Guard—a fat, torpid, pasty caricature of a man, Corporal Pudgy Squishbottom—were also quizzing people: "What is your fourth General Order?" "Who is the Sergeant Major of the Marine Corps?" "During what battle did the Marines earn the nickname *Devil Dog?*" My own private but desperate answers were, "You've got me by the short-n-curlies," "Who cares?" and "the Battle of Belleau Wood." I had been a Marine for almost five years—and yet I felt like I was in boot camp again.

The moment approached, like an execution, or at least a trial, as they were finishing the inquisition of the second rank. My boots? Well, yeah, you could see a little black on them, especially the right one which didn't have so much dust. My hair? Okay, so I hadn't had it cut in a month. My goatee grew in naturally from lack of cheek hairs. Of *course* my uniform was freshly withdrawn from the bottom of my seabag: I had just moved.

"Boy, you look like you been hit with a wrinkle-stick. You just pull that uniform out of your seabag?"

I was speechless.

"Never mind. *Inspection Harms!*"

"Damned right it does."

The snorts of laughter around me were reassuring.

"I said, *Inspection Harms!*" Sergeant Small demanded again.

I just shrugged and handed him my rifle. With a slow, incredulous drawl, he asked, "What's your name, Marine?"

"Uh . . . *Turnipseed?*"

"Uh-huh. What nationality is that, *Vegetable?*"

"I think it's a translation. German. But it really is Turnipseed. Honest."

"Okay, well—fuck, Turnipseed, how long you been in the Marine Corps?"

"Four and a half years—or so."

"And you're a lousy lance corporal?"

"Well, you know, I've been corporal a few times."

"All right, so you're a real smart type. Well, let me ask you this, you're so smart, What's your seventh General Order?"

"To learn the other ten?"

For me, guard duty will always be associated with shitbirds. A shitbird may be a rebel, or even a clown, but is always a loser—defunct, even when hiding behind a mask of irony. When I was eighteen, and stationed at Camp Johnson in lovely Jacksonville, North Carolina, I was put on guard duty for being a shitbird when I was supposed to be a role model. I had been an honor graduate in boot camp, and had been meritoriously promoted. My buddy Dave's dad had been a Marine Corps drill instructor during Vietnam, and had been the master sergeant in charge of recruiting in Minneapolis when Dave and I enlisted. I always thought that he had a Hitchcockian presence in everything I did in the Marines, a hidden hand in every success.

And I fucked it all up. The '86 World Series was on while I was at Camp Johnson. Seems I had decided to partake in a drinking game, innocent really, around a TV in a Jacksonville hotel room. Depending on our team loyalty, we each had to drink a beer for each run the opposing team scored. My team was the Miracle Mets, no shabby substance abusers themselves. Unfortunately, this wager was placed during game two which was pitched by Clemens for Boston and in which Gooden, Aquilera (6th), Orosco (7th), Fernandez (9th), and Sisk (9th) would receive a combined shelling for eighteen runs on behalf of the Mets.

My pals deposited me, completely pissed, in my barracks room bed after the game. Unbeknownst to me, I decided to take myself and my cotton briefs into the shower. With the shower door open. Seems the firewatch saw a suspicious stream of water coming out from beneath my door and investigated.

Fifteen minutes later, the MPs kicked the bathroom door in to let a Navy Corpsman administer smelling salts. My first reaction was to punch the corpsman in the nose, which, given the ammoniac strength of his salts and the depths of my drunkenness, barely amounted to tit for tat. I was joined, shortly, by Spiller and DeBeer, my roommates from Missouri and Upper Michigan, respectively. They were freshly arrived from tattoos and a fight at a cowboy bar in town. Then an ambulance pulled up outside our barracks along with two MP squad cars. For whatever reason, two other Marines had decided to get into a knock-down, drag-out, tooth-loosening brawl on the sidewalk outside my room. Spiller hopped up to share DeBeer's rack while the brawlers sat bleeding and handcuffed on his rack. I tried to get dressed between dry heaves. As I struggled to walk the halls of the hospital, I dry heaved into every available push-button ashtray I could find.

As it turned out, our adventures were nothing. There had been a squadbay-destroying race riot that night as well. So when the master gunnery sergeant called me into his office the Monday following, I was surprised when he pulled a Ka-Bar from his drawer and plunged it a half-inch deep into his desk.

"If you want to kill yourself, Marine, why don't you do it like a man?"

"But I don't want to kill myself. I just want the Mets to win the World Series."

"Don't fuck with me. You're a drunk. A coward. A pussy. You're a real shitbird who doesn't care about his God, his Country, his Corps—not even his worthless-fucking-self. I ought to kill you myself, you piece of shit."

I just stared at him. I was eighteen. I hadn't had a beer in six months before that crazy night. I had placed a stupid bet. I was training for college. He seemed awfully and unnecessarily wound up. He placed me on guard duty every weekend for six months. Even though I was later given a Meritorious Mast for placing first in my class at mechanic's school, and made corporal within two years of graduating from boot camp, my enthusiasm for the Marine Corps never recovered.

The worst of my six-month guard stint was Thanksgiving, during which I learned the true meaning of shitbird. It rained the entire four days of our ninety-six. I stood guard, four on, eight off, the entire weekend. I was on a walking post, at a Motor-T lot out by the Officers' Club. Cold November winds howled through the scrub pines. It didn't entirely suck, however, since I managed several hours half-sleep each shift in the Hummers, eyes open for any movement in the shadows or for lights coming down the road. But the poor unnamed bastard in the Chicken Coop . . .

The Chicken Coop was the camp armory. In the middle of a forty-by-forty foot square of dust surrounded by a tall, barbed-wire fence stood a garden shack containing a few dozen M-16's and Beretta 9 mm pistols. If you were assigned to the Chicken Coop, you spent four hours walking in a small circle in the middle of Camp Johnson. The stocks at Plymouth Colony would have been better—there you could rest. Well, during that particular weekend there was an artist assigned to the Chicken Coop. A guy so desperate and forlorn that it was a stroke of genius to assign him. He turned his assignment to the Chicken Coop into performance art. One day he walked it without boots—barefoot. Another day, he periodically stopped, leaned over, and farted toward the guard shack. He attracted an audience:

"What a fucking shitbird."

"You're a disgrace."

"Get out of my Corps, you fucking faggot."

On the last day, he put on a bravura performance: he snuck a long-neck Budweiser, then locked himself in the Chicken Coop, sat down with his legs splayed lazily in the dust, drank his Bud, and fell asleep with his hand down his pants, cupping his balls.

He was the high priest, the avatar, the Platonic ideal of shitbirds.

I hadn't been on guard duty since—and so much had happened in those four long years. Now I was scrambling to learn my general orders as I unpacked. About a half-dozen of us were new to the shift, and we put our gear away while the old pros relaxed in their cots and cynicism. While on my way to the guard shack, I had scored a couple of ammunition crates made of thin boards stapled together, like shallow apple crates. Using the butt of my Ka-Bar, I nailed these to a stud next to my bunk. Above the shelves I pounded one nail for my helmet, and another for my gas mask. Someone had already placed a nail at a handy height for my rifle, and next to it a nail for my shaving kit. There was an endless racket as cots got stretched onto their frames, Ka-Bars pounded nails into tent-frames, and neighbors became acquainted. My neighbors were Memphis, a quiet black guy with a mousy voice; Milwaukee, a young, often unshaven radio repairman whose throbbing headphones never ceased; Boston, a plumber and a plumber's son who had this laugh-cough following every sentence: "That's a real piece of work you got there, Lance Corporal. Huh-huh." Then there was Todd, whose cot was adjacent to mine: during the first hour of my unpacking, he remained supine and completely silent, with his mouth pursed in chagrin.

I looked up at them. "What?"

"You brought all them books over here to a *war?*" asked Boston.

"Yeah, what're you, some kind of nut?" asked Milwaukee.

Todd, still silent, rolled his eyes and plopped back down on his pillow, groaning in disbelief.

I got up off the floor and sat on the edge of my cot, looking at him. "Hey, you know Satan fell by force of gravity?"

"So did Newton's apple," Todd answered, "You think Newton would've been stupid enough to haul half a library through the middle of the desert?"

"He was an *alchemist* and *kabbalist*—of course he would have. Besides, this is only a small fraction of my library."

"You're not helping your case."

"What's your name?"

"Todd. How 'bout yours?"

"Joel."

"You're Turnipseed, right?"

"Yeah."

"Figures you'd be a goof. Everyone at the ISMO had a real chuckle when your name came across the database. You're in Motor T, right?"

"How'd you know?"

"We know everything at ISMO—where we bend over backward to serve you, 'cause if we bent over forward, we'd get fucked."

"ISMO?"

Todd plopped back down on his cot.

Sergeant Small entered the tent, dragging a smirking Squishbottom behind.

"Let's get out and onto the five-ton, Marines. Except you, Turnipseed, I've got a real special post for you. You wait here while we drive everyone around the port and show them to their posts."

Camp Shepard with its guard shack, Motor Transport, Supply, ISMO, MP shacks and shelter for all other Marines in Jubayl—was a quarter-mile by one-mile expanse of olive-drab GP Mediums, aligned rank and file, broken only by the few larger tents housing the various company offices, by the Conex railcar boxes in which the post office and other high-security services were housed, by the great outdoor theater made of whitewashed plywood, with sandbags stacked around the plywood-and-two-by-four bleachers just in case Saddam Hussein decided to drop a SCUD between reels. Next to Camp Shepard was the naval hospital, itself a large expanse of green tents wrapped in silvery blankets of Tyvek insulation. Across the street were the Army and their Patriot missile batteries, all housed in yet another unbroken expanse of uniform green tents.

About the only thing that wasn't housed in a green tent or a green railroad box was the small compound at the intersection of several of the port roads. One trailer housed the barbershop. Another housed the PX's check-cashing center. There was one trailer that served pizza and cheeseburgers. This is the trailer that could appear completely desolate from several blocks' distance, but as you approached, miraculously grew a line of twenty people from ten different armed services.

If you walked out the heavily bunkered and well-manned gates of Camp Shepard and crossed the street, you stepped into this olive-drab strip mall; a semi-surburban paradise. If you crossed the next street beyond, you came to two large, H-shaped white buildings, several stories tall. Headquarters.

I was assigned to the Headquarters building closest to Camp Shepard. After a few cigarettes' solitude, Sergeant Small returned to our tent to walk me over to my post. He explained that our shifts would run four hours on, eight hours off for five consecutive days, at which point we would stand a twenty-four-hour REACT team shift—responsible for any security emergencies at the port—and then have twenty hours off until our next rotation, during which each shift would begin four hours earlier than the previous rotation.

My regular post was in the first-floor lobby of the building: a large plywood counter lined, inside and out, with sandbags. When I sat down behind the counter I could barely see over it, which made me look like Kilroy—nose, eyes, and helmet rising above the ledge. The sun poured in through the glass doors and wall-high windows, casting long shadows behind the sparse white pillars. This post-Beirut interior decor and International Style architecture were, by themselves, enough to induce despair.

I spent most of my first shift trying to figure out whether Sergeant Small actually respected me, or whether I got this post because the officers wandering in and out of Headquarters could keep an eye on me.

The first officer I was called upon to salute was the chaplain, who raised his limp hand halfway up his face, then let it flop back down to his side. Sergeant Small's instruction to salute "like a Marine" betrayed itself as silly: how could I take seriously a man who looked like he was wearing a bad glue-on mustache?

"Hey, look who's here," he said, "it's the third-person Marine. Or shall I call you 'the philosopher?'"

"Well, *the* Philosopher was Aristotle. Dante, remember?"

"Yes, and I think Aquinas called Aristotle '*the* Philosopher' as well. Did you start this post today?"

"About an hour ago, and Boethius informed both Dante and Aquinas of Aristotle, right?"

"Of course, *The Consolations of Philosophy*," he said. "Written in jail, I believe." He looked at his watch. "Looks like you've got plenty of time to *tarry*."

"I hope that doesn't mean you want me to pray."

We both laughed.

"Looks as though you're getting plenty done," he said, setting a stack of books down on the heavily graffitoed counter. "Are you writing your own *Consolations?*"

I blushed, picking up the worn sheet of paper in front of me.

"Well, sir, to be honest, I'm not supposed to be reading on post. General Orders."

"Which General Order is that—'no reading on post'?"

"I don't think it is one. Not that I'd know. It's the *General Orders* I'm studying."

Between shifts Todd and I talked about my books, cracked jokes about the moronic behavior of Boston and Milwaukee, had dinner at the chow hall—always an adventure—and talked about the early days of Operation Desert Shield.

"Yeah," he said, "I knew something was up as early as June. We packed up the ISMO at Pendleton and shipped out to Florida to do these exercises: we set up comm lines and computer networks just like it was Saudi and Kuwait. Same places, same roads, everything. It was like déjà vu all over again when we got to the real Saudi."

"How long have you been here?"

"Oh man, we got here in like, August. Shit, we were the first ones off the plane. ISMO always is."

"Okay, I can't take it any more," I said, "What's ISMO?"

"You know, we do networking and programming, databases . . . stuff like that so you guys are less fucked up. Of course, you're always fucked up anyway, but we do the best we can to unfuck you."

"Who's 'we'? I mean, who's fucked up?"

"Everyone in the Marine Corps except us. Look, you're Motor T, right?"

"Yeah. How'd you know?"

"Like I said, I saw your name come up on the manifests. Bravo Company, Sixth Motor Transport Battalion. You're all reservists who got called up to drive the semis. You got here about two weeks ago, and your staff and officers couldn't do paperwork properly if their dicks were pens and pussy was paper."

"So, you're, like, Big Brother?"

"Not really. Mostly I drink Coke and fuck around playing Sim City with Tex. I just replaced him on guard duty. Can you believe it? Best friends and we hardly get to see each other for a month."

"Yeah, well, my best friend is sitting in a coffee shop in Minneapolis," I said. "You've been here since August?"

"Since August. You wouldn't believe what idiots the officers were when we got here. They'd pull their pistols out if you shook your dick too many times in the head—like an Iraqi was waiting inside your boxers or something. Assholes."

"Yeah, the word in the rumor mill is that the war hasn't started yet because the Army wasn't even ready until January."

"The Army? Shit, the only part of the Marine Corps that was ready was the ISMO. We were done in two weeks, from Riyadh to Mishab—laid out and online."

"Nobody else was ready?"

"Everybody else was scared shitless. If Saddam was smart, he'd have overrun us in September. He'd have kicked our ass. This place was one hundred percent fucked up, a total clusterfuck. They had us living in those warehouses, and it was like a hundred degrees in the shade, with flies in everything. They'd have us in formations every other hour to see if anyone was missing yet. Then they'd march us around with loaded rifles to patrol the port. What a joke. I want to get back to Pendleton and do something useful."

"Like what?"

"Tex and I are teaching each other c and c++. When I get out of the Corps, I want to move back to Oregon and start making some real money."

After dinner, Todd and I returned to our tent to fashion a prop for my post: a sign to place on my counter. When I returned to my post that evening, I put it up:

PHILOSOPHY OF THE DAY—FIVE CENTS' WORTH

The Soldiers made on me the impression, not of many individuals, but of one vast centipede of a man, good for all sorts of pulling down; and why not then for some kinds of building up? If men could combine thus earnestly, and patiently, and harmoniously to some really worthy end, what might they not accomplish? They now put their hands, and partially perchance their heads together, and the result is that they are the imperfect tools of an imperfect and tyrannical government. But if they could put their hands and heads and hearts all together, such a co-operation and harmony would be the very end and success for which government now exists in vain— a government, as it were, not only with tools, but stock to trade with.

Henry Thoreau, "A Yankee in Canada"

It had only been a month since I'd gotten the call, but the nine-page letter I got from Mark one afternoon made it seem like years. He quoted from Kierkegaard and Nietzsche and Emerson, mixing in his own ruminations:

The Mundane: I am struck by the amount of time wasted in "civil" life. The sense of urgency that surrounds daily activity is limited to the petty and the mundane. Undoubtedly there are more things by which one can occupy their time, yet to what end? Shall I strike an arabesque: my perfect repose? Is my paint my life in thought and deed, each day my canvas, my existence an exhibit? What critique will you offer its entirety; not the one or the few which is exceptional by mere chance, but the whole of it? Here is man's great dilemma: that his capacity for virtue is equally matched by his ca-

pacity for degradation. Is it not evident that the artisan's arabesque may
be inspired by the highest ideals just as much as the lowest?

I've got Boston and Milwaukee talking beer farts and pussy, Sergeant Small busting my balls about Inspection Arms and the General Orders for Sentries, and seven thousand miles away, Mark is still talking to me like I'm a transcendentalist. What the fuck? If I was going to be a hero of anything, it was going to be as camp smart-ass and champion smoker of two eighty-five-cent packs of Camels a day. I had lost myself and didn't know what to make for a metaphor: like a book misshelved on the stacks; like a grain of sand in the desert; like what? Like nothing but what I was—another Marine in camouflage carrying a rifle and a pack with a radio.

In Saudi Arabia. In the port of Al Jubayl. On guard duty. On REACT patrol. Our truck parked in the sand just inside the main gate. We piled off the bed into a long column. Diesel fumes mixed with the salt from the Gulf. A hundred yards behind us, trucks pulled to a stop at the MP shacks. The drivers handed their papers down from the cab, then disappeared into the night like an intermittent stream of slow tracers, red and orange and yellow trailer lights heading toward their targets near the Iraqi and Kuwaiti borders.

Bound by silence, we began marching along the fence surrounding the port. The blades of the concertina wire glistened above us. In the distance, the burnoff from the gas-oil separation facilities rose in sporadic dances of fire. Immediately beyond the fence lay Jubayl: four- and five-story cement apartments with Islamic arches, some only half-completed; a dog rummaging through trash cans; alleys filled with litter and the occasional sedan parked at an angle to the curb. Only the static crackle of the radio and the annoying knock of the antenna against my helmet broke the tired quiet of our steps, which dragged through loose sand and scuffled across concrete.

I hadn't had a smoke since our rude awakening by Sergeant Small and his nightstick. I couldn't bring myself to believe that there was an actual incident awaiting our reaction. If a round had gone off, it was probably one of the sentries shooting a dog beyond the fence, just for kicks. "Hey, man, I was just, you know, checking to see that there wasn't any sand in my bolt. I couldn't believe it when it went off. Like, holy shit, I didn't have the safety on or anything." That kind of thing. I wasn't even thinking when I pulled a smoke from my flak jacket and lit it.

"Are you fucking crazy?" someone whispered. "Put that thing out, pal."

Fifty feet ahead, the lead men of our patrol were walking beneath a spotlight, squad formation on stage. Someone smacked the back of my pack. I turned around to see the sergeant of the guard, the real one, whose full-time job it was to supervise the guard rotations. He was a hand-chiseled black guy. Rumor had it that he had recently flunked out of drill instructor's school. Didn't look like he'd flunked to me.

"What the fuck is this?" he asked, eyeballs about three inches away from the glowing cherry of my cigarette. An answer seemed superfluous. The whispering guy ahead of me answered anyway.

"It's a cigarette."

No shit. Now I was standing in the spotlight, my radio antenna waving high above. The flunked DI was looking at my flak jacket collar for rank, the chevron with crossed rifles that I had never bothered to put on.

"What's your name, private?"

I answered like I had just been requisitioned from Marine Corps Supply, "Lance Corporal, Turnipseed, Joel. One each."

I had long since stepped my cigarette into the sand.

"You some kind of comedian?"

I could hear Todd laugh in the distance. Milwaukee and Boston, too. I thought of the Chicken Coop.

"Look, we're standing here beneath fifty-thousand-watt lights. It's no big deal."

"Yeah," he said, "Well, we'll just see how big a deal it is, Turnipseed. You come talk to me tomorrow morning, 'cause you're mine now, Lance Corporal."

A truck was waiting for us a few hundred yards down the fence, right next to the warehouse on whose roof Post Four was located. We climbed in to double back to the front gate, where we would start again and patrol the coast. My cigarette and I bounced in the back of the five-ton. Our stares focused about an inch from our faces, inward gazes of exhaustion and boredom. I never did go see him.

The entire coastline was covered with rocks ranging in size from a fist to a Volkswagen. Here the PRC-47 really lived up to its nickname: the Prick. Heads disappeared behind rocks, then rose again, swaying along uncertain steps. The lone sentry in the machine-gun nest looking out over the Gulf stared at us from behind his camouflage netting. *0200: Crazy motherfuckers coming downrange.* Ahead of us the cranes of the port rose above the silhouettes of ships, red lights flashing against their white paint. We walked past Saudi Motors, where the yellow light in the window of the dispatch trailer, juxtaposed with the slow waves of the Gulf, formed a comforting admixture of loneliness and freedom.

When we arrived at Camp Shepard, creeping up on the tents from the sea, everything seemed deserted. It was as if we were walking through an empty movie set. We moved among the tents in squad formation, not speaking. Sergeant Small used hand signals: arm rotating backwards with the palm extended, to form a column; arms extended to the sides, then brought forward, to close up; raised arm brought down and rotated to the side, to disperse through the tent camp. Todd and I ducked out behind the showers, then walked to the chow hall. The crew hadn't arrived yet, and the frying pans, spoons, strainers, and cannibal-sized pots glistened in the moonlight as they hung from their pegs. We caught sight of Sergeant Small again in a clearing out by the warehouses in which ISMO was headquartered. He was beckoning silently, giving us the rally point sign: touching his belt, then pointing to the ground while circling with his hand. I half-expected to hear a director somewhere yell "Cut!" then have a smoke while watching the crew pack their cameras. I felt like I was an actor in my own life—and I was playing the role of shitbird.

Intelligence

IN THE MORNINGS, the sun blazed through the glass doors of Head-quarters. Whenever one of the doors opened, it caught a direct reflection, burning my pupils to thin points. Toward the end of one shift, my eyes slowly resolved into focus a small, balding man with little round glasses. It was the gunny from S-2, Marine Corps Intelligence. He set a black D-ring binder on the plywood of my bunker-desk-booth-thing.

"Just about six, Lance Corporal. You gettin' off soon?"

"Yup, two to six," I replied. "You're here early. Or late, I'm not sure which."

He and I had struck up a kind of hallway friendship, as I had with the chaplain and one of the captains in the MP unit.

"I've got a lot of reports to clean up. Lots of work right now . . . " he said, letting his words trail off suggestively. "Say there, Lance Corporal, I've been thinkin' of that sign of yours, the Thoreau quotation you're always puttin' up? It really got me to puzzle over things . . . I like that."

"That's great. What did it make you think about?"

"*Bartlett's Quotations*. There's this General Sherman quotation in there." He paused for a moment to stick his chest out ever so slightly, tilting his head back, as if modelling himself after the Lyceum style of Everett and Webster. "War is at best barbarian," the gunny said. "Its glory is all moonshine. It is only those who have neither fired a shot nor heard the shrieks and groans of the wounded who cry aloud for blood, more vengeance, more desolation. War is hell."

"That's a remarkable thing to hear from the man who made Georgia howl, isn't it?" I remarked.

"Not really. He could only know it *because* he had burned the South. It's kind of like the tragedy of tragedy or something—you can't warn other people until you've become a hero for doing the thing you're warning the other people about."

I was nonplussed. "Sort of like a reverse or obverse 'Chicken Little,' right?"

"Exactly! Sort of like the Marines. I was a history major, you know, at North Carolina—"

"Good school. Great hoops."

"Great city. Raleigh-Durham–Chapel Hill—I love that place. Anyway, I was a history major till my wife got pregnant. I joined the Marines. Went Intel. Got divorced. Lived in Korea, Philippines, Japan, Saudi Arabia, Germany, Norway. I tell my nephew, 'Hey, don't join the Marines. Go to college, for Christ's sake.' But he doesn't listen. He can't believe that the *adventure* wears you down and kills you. Smoke too much, swear too damn much . . ."

I continued, adding to the list, "No one to talk to when you get excited about something, no good foreign movies on base, shit-hole towns to live in. No cappuccino. Everyone and everything is coarse, debauched . . ."

He was staring at the guard-booth graffiti when I ended my litany. "You're in philosophy?" he asked, looking up.

"Yeah. Philosophy, and maybe classics. I don't know. I just like to read and think, the school part always seems secondary."

"Don't let it become secondary, or you'll end up a forty-year-old gunny reading the most god-awfully boring reports you've ever seen while drinking coffee that tastes like old pennies and smells like unleaded. Cappuccino? Finish your fucking degree."

"Okay, if you say so."

"And come up to my office. Have a cup of coffee, I'll make it fresh. I'll show you the Intelligence life from the inside."

"All right. But I don't get off till six—is that okay?"

"It's great. I'll be there waiting with a fresh cup of joe."

After being relieved, I walked up the stairs to the second floor. For two weeks I had watched people disappear up the stairs, wondering where they were going; what wonders of modern technology they sat down to when they went to work at spying and surveillance. Some days I pictured a minimalist Scandanavian decor—white rooms with pine trim. On others I thought like Terry Gilliam—air-driven delivery tubes in plexiglass chutes, computers, radars, printers, medieval mechanisms of torture, test tubes, photographic developing stations, all secreted in dirt-pink LED shadows.

When I arrived at the top of the stairs, I found that the second floor resembled the first: the dull, lesser-imitation Bauhaus architecture with which governments and hospitals have been hung over since the thirties. The gunny was sitting in front of his computer, typing away like a veteran secretary or paperback novelist, a cigarette smoldering in an ashtray beside the keyboard.

"Excuse me," I asked, standing in the doorway. "Am I still invited for a cup of coffee?"

"Hey, Lance Corporal! Come in, come in. Have a seat." He got up cheerfully, leaving his office chair spinning lazily behind him.

I walked in, tentatively, looking at the desk next to the gunny's.

"Oh, hell, that's all right, sit at the captain's desk. He won't be around until nine. Let me make that coffee." He began poking around in the office, talking into the walls as he looked over the shelves. "Put away that canteen cup, I've got a fresh cup around here somewhere. Fresh coffee, too. How was your shift?"

"Fine. Boring."

He disappeared, out of the office and around the corner. On the captain's desk, a bulky dot-matrix printer began to exorcise itself of a report. *Screeench. Clickety—clickety—clack—clickety. Clack—clack—clickety—claaaack—clack. Screeench.* Line after line it wailed its mechanical paroxysms.

"Look who's here," said the gunny as he stepped back into the office, pointing a Mr. Coffee carafe full of swirling yellow water at the printer, "it's the morning Intelligence Summary. Noisy bitch, isn't she?"

A long, angular stream of paper stretched to the floor, folding for a few pages, then arching up in protest and spilling out further onto the linoleum.

"That's one hell of a report," I commented.

"Yeah, and I have to condense several of them every day. Can you imagine?" he said, deftly picking up the stream of pages, folding them into a perfectly perforated stack.

"That's pretty good," I said. " I could never do that with printer paper, it always catches. Do you have to read all of that? Or is there just some place you can look for the most relevant information?"

He had already begun scanning the pages, flipping them one over the other. "Sure, I read all of it. You can't be prejudiced, or you might miss a significant pattern. You know, like absences might be as significant as appearances. Hey, go ahead and smoke. I won't tell anyone."

I wondered if *he* knew that I smoked while on post? Maybe he saw one of the other guys—we all smoked. His office was no different from any other Marine Corps office: green steel desks with green steel chairs, sickly beige four-drawer file cabinets—atop which stood framed pictures of a teenaged boy, and a Filipino woman holding a daughter in her lap, and between them, a potted ivy. Framed promotion warrants and school certificates hung on the wall above the desks, a calendar, and a "Stay Marine" recruiting poster displaying a Marine in sprinter's stance morphed into a red Ferrari. A shelf opposite the desks was crammed with technical manuals and Marine Corps Institute course books, a few dirty cups, a crusty Coffee-Mate jar and a Mr. Coffee machine, as well as more ivy plants competing for space. Did they bring *potted plants* with them to the Gulf?

"Say, Gunny, is that your ex-wife up there?"

"The Filipino? No, that's my *wife*. I got remarried a few years ago. Isn't my daughter gorgeous? They live in Oceanside right now. I wish I could afford to move them out of there. I'm going to retire in two years. I should be a master sergeant by then, that'll give us a good retirement. I'd like to move back to North Carolina."

"You going to finish *your* degree?"

"No. No, I've got a pretty good nest egg. I think I'll buy a little house, and a boat, and try and write myself a Tom Clancy or Jim Webb novel. I've seen enough for that. Want to see what happened last night while you were downstairs philosophizing?"

He handed me the stack of papers. I glanced out the open door.

"It's okay," he said, "go ahead, check it out."

"All right," I replied, taking the papers from him, "is it interesting?"

"Depends on what you bring to it," he said, pouring coffee. "If you know how to read it, it is. I'm interested to see what you make of it."

"I'll ask if I find anything beyond my ken," I said.

He handed me a stoneware mug that weighed about five pounds and went back to his computer.

"Boy," I remarked after reading a few pages, "we sure didn't hit much last night, did we?"

"Never do," he said. I didn't look up again for a long time, engrossed by the unending stream of information, mysterious and mostly unintelligible:

MISSION 427 0402 KTO 29.46N 46.48E BDA: NO DAMAGE

MISSION 428 0404 KTO 29.47N 46.46E BDA: T-55

MISSION 429 0404 KTO 29.47N 46.48E BDA: NO DAMAGE

MISSION 430 0414 KTO 30.68N 44.45E BDA: NO REPORT

MISSION 431 0416 KTO 30.68N 44.46E BDA: NO DAMAGE

And the list continued through several cigarettes and more pages: NO DAMAGE; NO DAMAGE; NO REPORT; NO DAMAGE. In the middle of the stack I came across a half-page summary:

CENTCOM UPDATE TO BDA——0430 13 FEB 1991

TANKS: 1368 (31%)

ARTILLERY: 825 (26%)

ARMORED PERSONNEL: 958 (34%)

PERSONNEL: 80,000 (13%)

IRAQI EFFECTIVENESS—KTO: 65%
***EST. FUEL STORES: 6 MONTHS
***EST. RATION STORES: 9 MONTHS
***EST POT. WATER STORES: 6 MONTHS

MORALE REPORTED BY IRAQI POW'S: EXTREMELY LOW

I looked up from the pale blue letters. The gunny was typing away like he was already at work on his first novel, smoothly and without interruption, only occasionally nibbling on the inside corner of his lips.

"Say, Gunny," I asked, "What do *you* think of all this?"

"All what?" he asked, still typing.

"Well, it seems to me like the Iraqis still have an awful lot of fighting capacity. Don't you think?"

"As far as materiel is concerned? Sure. But half the sorties we fly these days don't drop anything but the best damned propaganda in the world—these poor fuckers, if they don't get shot from behind first, are going to come out from their holes voting Republican."

I laughed. "Really?"

"Yeah, *really*. You of all people should know that *that*'s what makes America the greatest superpower on the planet: brainwashing. America is the first country to govern itself on the principle that no one wants to die for a cause, but we are all dying to live for one. Which is fine: the same art used to keep everyone happy and lazy against the normal human drives for expression and fulfillment is also powerful enough to keep them angry and ready to fight against the normal human drives for propagation and preservation. Wisdom may rest in the mean, but America is about the successful exploitation of the extremes. And people the world over are beginning to resonate with this program. It works."

"Are you sure you're a Marine?" I asked.

"Yeah. But I'm a *cynical* Marine."

A pall of silence broke the spirit of our conversation. He shrugged and returned to his typing, somehow managing to light a cigarette without missing a beat.

"Go ahead, keep reading. There's nothing disheartening in *there*."

MISSION 462 Ø51Ø KTO 3Ø.4ØN 45.46E BDA: TK ARTILLERY

MISSION 463 Ø51Ø KTO 3Ø.4ØN 45.46E BDA: NO DAMAGE

MISSION 464 Ø511 KTO 3Ø.41N 45.48E BDA: NO DAMAGE

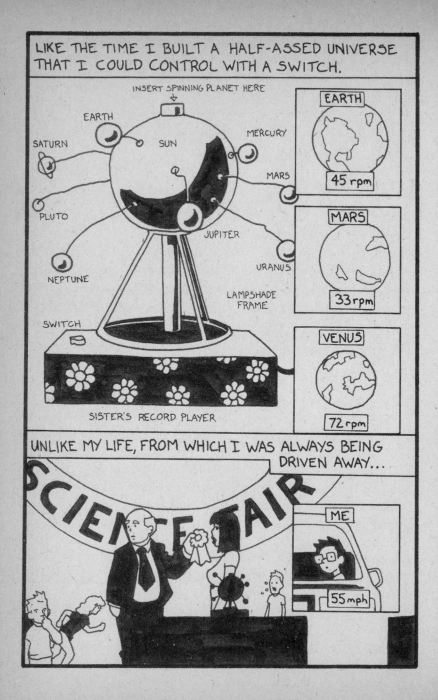

Solitude

I have concluded that all of man's troubles have one cause,
that he cannot sit still in a room by himself.

Pascal

FUCKIN' A, RIGHT.

I was standing post at the loneliest hour of night, the two-to-six A.M. shift. I floated in the faint glow of grey light from the hallway, spreading coolly across the shimmering tile floors. Floated in greys and thalo blues and also in the pale cadmium red of the EXIT sign, my attention lost in the faint radio crackle of the MP station, a mesmerizing drone that died a crisp but quiet death as its waves bounced invisibly against the cement walls.

This is the sort of solitude Pascal was talking about. No pacing, for that brings in the world. No murmuring, muttering, puttering. No reading. This is the sort of solitude whose acceptance is a poetic or religious act. Or is a sign of an utter lack of inner resources, a solitude often, if not best, spent drunk.

Lights reflected in broad, circular bands in the plate-glass windows at which I stared, lights from outside and from a distance. I couldn't see anything beyond glass, its shadows and reflections. It would be hours before anyone left their office to go to the head, or before someone entered the building to get an early start. There would be no one with whom to chat, or for whom I had to stand up and salute. I was alone.

So this is where we go down in the volcano with the mothers; wrestle with our demons; bear our torments. The action doesn't match the verbs, let me just tell you.

I was standing there, rifle over my shoulder, thinking again about the time I got beat up in fourth grade because I didn't believe in God, or about the time I laughed when the girlfriend I had just broken up with drove away with so much piss and vinegar that she crashed her car at thirty miles an hour into the dumpster of the Chinese restaurant in the alley beneath my campus apartment, spilling vegetable peelings and fish bones all over the hood of her car. So we remember shit. Dreams, too, I suppose.

A door closed down the long hallway and around the corner, a quiet click and reminder of humanity in the uncoverable distance. I shifted my feet and checked my rifle. My helmet pressed with a deep ache into my skull, an ache that echoed within. That was the deal with the Kevlar helmets—they presented you with two unsatisfactory choices: you could tighten the strap inside to prevent the helmet from resting on the top of your head, but that cut the circulation off to your ears, which, along with your neck, tingled before going numb; or you could let a ten-pound helmet rest on a growing knot on top of your skull—a sort of perma-noogie. It's the sort of design the Marine Corps might have specified to the manufacturer: "Say, can you design the helmet, combat, Kevlar, M-2, to give a sort of constant noogie to the troops? Keeps 'em from getting into mischief." Not unlike, as I remembered it there on post, the season my father decided to spank all the kids each morning before leaving for work—we'd deserve it during the day anyway, right? This is the logic of "Fucker!" and "Bitch!" and "I hate you!" and "You hit me like that again and I'll break your fucking wrists, you bitch!" and "Fuck you, you little prick, you're not my son!" And this is the logic of my dreams.

I pulled a cigarette out of my pocket without letting the package show, without letting the cigarette show, cupping it delicately in my hand . . . my Zippo I lit beneath the lip of the counter so that no telling reflection could appear in the plate glass. Just in case. I sat on the folding chair, leaning forward in a huddle over the cigarette. I took a long, deep drag, burning the cherry to a long bright point beneath a shroud of flaky ash. I held it for as long as I could, letting the smoke settle in my lungs, exhaling in a long, rushed whisper in whose substance I could barely detect the presence of smoke. I stubbed the cigarette up beneath the counter, wiping the ash off with a corner of my shirt. I ground the fallen embers and black ashes into the loose sand on the tiles. My ALICE pack lay open against the bulging sandbags, and into it I tossed the spent cigarette before resuming my stare out into the night.

This is where I fought much of my war. In silence. At two A.M. on a guard post or three A.M. out on the highway hauling a load of 155 mm shells. Alone. Without guns.

An hour later, when dawn broke and the corporal of the guard came to relieve me he asked, "You been smokin' back there, Lance Corporal?"

"No," I replied, "no, I haven't."

He looked at me with glint-eyed suspicion. "That right?" he asked, pausing to let his gaze sink in. "Don't think I don't have you all figured out. I know what you up to—I know what you all about, Lance Corporal. You think you special, but you ain't shit." I just stared at him. He paused again, this time clicking his tongue against the roof of his mouth, looking off into the distance. "You're relieved," he said, raising his hand as if shooing away a dog.

The Dog Pound

IT WAS ONLY a couple hundred yards from the guard tent to the Motor Transport Battalion's tents, but I stumbled beneath packs weighing more than I did. I carried three seabags, one like a backpack and one over each shoulder, my rifle in one hand and a cot in the other. With this load I struggled around and beside and between tents. I stumbled over ropes and chains, the cement blocks to which they were attached, past stray pallets and bars and posts and beams jutting out from beneath the moldy canvas. I stepped around piss puddles, half-opened and discarded packets of Chicken à la King MREs looking like vomit: white and curdled with peas and carrots.

I stumbled forward, peeking into each tent as I walked past, checking for an open space to drop my bags and stretch my cot. The Marines inside the first tent I checked out had pushed their cots to the edges of the tent. They sat like rustlers around the Bunsen burner in the center. A pot of soup boiled above the flames. They turned as one to look at me, staring, extending their arms—"Go to hell, this is our tent."

It was hot, Saudi Arabia hot.

Sweat ran down my forehead and into my eyes, my glasses riding the salty beads to the end of my nose. I had no hand to tip them up, and so inched through Camp Shepard looking foolish and absurd. I felt lost in a familiar landscape. The Minneapolis guys had moved north, to Mishab. Since the reserve units from Marine Wing Support Group 47 belonged to the First Marine Expeditionary Force, First Field Service Support Group, Sixth Motor Transport Battalion now, there were no Minneapolis tents to move into. In fact, there was no longer a Minneapolis unit—our home town was treated as an accident of origin, not an essential quality of daily life. The guys from Minneapolis had all been detached to the Seventh Motor Transport Battalion. In the ever-expanding grid of tents numbered simply by column and row, housing everyone from truckers to cooks to MPS to supply personnel to software developers, I couldn't even tell which tents belonged to our motor transport unit.

I was alone.

A voice, high, smooth, mellow and inviting—*mellifluous*—called out, "Hey brother, you lookin' for a place to live?"

My eyes spoke for me.

"Look no further, brother. Lemme help you with your trash. Name's Morris, but you can call me Mountain Man."

I gawked at him. Five-foot-three and bearded. A very well-trimmed, and very *non-regulation,* beard. It was a GI Joe with a Kung-Fu grip beard. Which is all I could think about, look at, as I was helped by the most effusively cheerful person I'd met in Saudi Arabia.

He carried two of my seabags into the tent.

"Lucky day," he said, "you got the corner spot."

"Thanks," I said, "Is this a Sixth Motor Transport Battalion tent?"

"Yes, sir. Best tent in the battalion, my brother. You just been moved into the Dog Pound," he said.

I sat on one of the seabags and began fishing for a cigarette. The tent smelled of pomade, Magic Shave, stinky feet, and sweat. There was a distant-memory-of-urine smell. A makeshift floor had been built from scrap pallets, and laundry was hanging above nearly every cot, criss-crossing the tent on lines going every which way, green shirts and socks hanging below a green tent and over the green sleeping bags draped over green cots, the black asphalt shining damp between the slats of the pallets. Shadows cast in every direction from the two open bulbs hanging high above. Except for me and Mountain Man, the tent was empty. Then he left. I smoked a cigarette before leaning back to sleep on my pile of seabags.

*   *   *

When I had awoken that morning, I was still on guard duty—lingering in half-sleep, anticipating the languorous pace of a four-on, eight-off day. Soft shadows enveloped our tent, and the frames of men lay still as they read, or lay sleeping in anticipation of a long night. Dancing dust particles held my attention as the sun beamed down through the holes in the tent. The beams were like spotlights illuminating a long-cancelled act. Sergeant Small stepped through the moldy flaps.

"Is Turnipseed in here?"

I moaned.

"Hey Turnipseed, yer s'posed to report back to yer unit today . . ." He paused, biting his lip. Todd rose from his cot. " . . . up North." My heart beat with a wild staccato flutter—my self momentarily dissolving into the random floating particles in the sunbeam before me. I blinked, injured.

"What time?" I asked.

"They just said today," he said.

I sat, and he stood. The seconds dragged out into a thousand considered possiblities. He stepped back out into the sunlight.

Up North. SCUD attacks, anthrax and mustard gas. It had only been two weeks since the Khafji invasion, the same two weeks that separated me from the Minneapolis Marines and Saudi Motors. With my eyes closed, the salt smell of the Gulf and the mildew of the tent and its men faded slowly as I pictured a wide-open stretch of road, stretching out through nothing but pounded sand, with nothing but the blue sky ahead and the white disk of the sun above. Hot. No clouds. Sweat pouring down my brow, filling the crack of my ass, sweat staining the cigarette resting between my fingers. And then nothing. I felt a release. Consumed in a plume of black smoke and fire, shattered glass and shredded steel. I opened my eyes to the dust still dancing before me—as though fear were not only palpable, but had just passed through me, leaving as quickly as it came, taking some weight with it.

Everyone in our half of the tent stared at me.

With packs on our backs, and rifles slung over our shoulders, Todd and I strolled past the machine-gun bunkers and out the gates of Camp Shepard. It was Valentine's Day, and we were headed for the new AT&T tent set up at the naval hospital. As we walked, I watched the soldiers maintaining the Patriot missile launchers, T-shirts rolled up to their flabby, pasty shoulders, cigarettes dangling from their lips, eyes squinted against the glare of the desert sun, or eyes absent behind Ray-Bans.

"Todd?" I asked, "Who are you going to call?"

"I don't know. My mom, probably. You going to call Sarah?"

"I would, but I don't know her number. I think maybe I'll just call my mom, too."

After the operator put the collect call through, I said, "Greetings from the land of a thousand lazy camels and a few dud SCUDs."

"Joel? Jesus, what time is it?"

"A little past one. In the afternoon. What does that make it in Minneapolis?"

"It's two-fifteen A.M."

"Oops. Well, it's still Valentine's Day, right? So here it is . . ." And on through our awkward conversation: she cried every day; she kept CNN tuned in, twenty-four/seven; she knew so much more about the war than I did, and told me all she knew. It was strange, like there were two separate wars going on, and they were reaching out to touch one another via satellite.

"What are you hearing from the States?" she asked.

"Mostly I'm just getting letters from you and Mark and the grandparents, and, of course, the *New Republic*. Mostly, after having been in Saudi Arabia for nearly a month, I am only just beginning to get mail at all."

"Have you heard from Sarah?"

"No. I was hoping you had heard something."

In the middle of my wallowing, I noticed that this guy was staring at me. He wasn't in line. I traced the bead of his overly solemn gaze, to a paper sign taped into the telephone stall:

ATTENTION: DO NOT GIVE AWAY VITAL INTELLIGENCE
Things which you are not allowed to say:
—How many people are living with you
—Kinds of equipment you have
—Where you have traveled
—What unit you are in
—Where you are
USE YOUR HEAD—DON'T GO HOME DEAD
All violations are subject to UCMJ and/or Court Martial

"Fuck it," I thought, "I'll tell her anyway."

"I forgot to tell you," I said, "I'm going to start driving again tomorrow. Also, I'll be moving up north. The rest of the guys from Minneapolis moved a couple weeks ago. A place called Al Mishab, I think. Same place that we heard shelling on our early runs, the ones we made right after we got here. Maybe you haven't gotten that letter yet."

She let out a three-in-the-morning moan.

"Listen," I told her, "I've been a Marine for almost five years now. I'll deal."

My idiot bravery woke her up, and we began to get into it. It wasn't hard for her: one minute, the ever-caring mother, the next she'd just bear down and grind me to death: "Did you know you haven't paid your student loans in three months? Did you know that you owe your landlord six hundred dollars? And Mark Durfee called to say he picked your books up from the bookstore—how can you buy books when you can't pay your student loans? Are you going to be a fuck-up your entire life?" Then the SCUD alarms begin whining.

"What's that noise in the background?"

"Just the city of Jubayl's SCUD alarm."

"Where's that from you?"

"About a thousand feet," I said, "But they set off their SCUD alarm if someone farts too loud in the mayor's office."

The whirling cries continued as the Saudi Coast Guard station added its defense sirens. I could barely hear her.

"Joel, please hang up. You can call me again. Go find a bunker or something. Joel?"

Todd is standing next to me now, chuckling. The Army cranks up *their* alarm. Then the Marine Corps.

"Jesus, Joel, that sounds like it's right next to you." I can hear the heave of breaths between sobs. I wish I could empathize, to soothe, to comfort or to care. But I've been up and down that roller coaster too many times.

Instead, I'm a smart-ass: "Next to me? I've got to duck every time the siren spins around."

Todd's face began to show the strain of waiting, and I decided I had better get going. "Well, Ma, love you lots and all that. Tell Sarah to write me a letter. Meanwhile, I've got a bunker to dive for."

Frantically, as though it were her last speech, my mother rattled off the litany of delinquent affections: "I love you, and I've always loved you, and everyone is praying for you, even if you don't believe in God, which you should, and Mikey and Carrie and Bill love you, even if they don't say it, and your father loves you . . . take care, I love you."

As soon as I hung up the sirens whirred to a stop. No SCUD. Nothing commensurate; everything out of whack. Including my friendship with Todd, which was about fifteen minutes from its end.

"You ready to go, Diogenes?" asked Todd. In our own version of whistling in the dark, we talked of Diogenes the Dog, not a Devil Dog, but a dog nonetheless—the original Cynic.

"One day," I told him, "when caught masturbating in the Agora, Diogenes was asked, 'Aren't you ashamed of yourself?' To which he replied, 'Ashamed? Are you kidding? I wish I could rub my stomach and make my hunger go away!'"

Our laughs punctuated the dying of the sirens, and we strode back toward Camp Shepard with rifles slung over our shoulders. We were laughing the laugh of cynics; the laugh of warriors. The laugh of friends who will never see each other again, caught in the divide of Marine Corps friendship, friends whose expectations derive in part from the whorehouse, but equally from the facts of bullets, artillery, and death.

* * *

I woke up on guard duty but now, in mid-afternoon, I was back in the Sixth Motor Transport Battalion. It's funny how much distance can be covered in six hours and a hundred fifty feet. I was still sitting on my cot, helmet cocked backward on my head, smoking a cigarette while taking acount of my new surroundings, when the Mountain Man reappeared.

"Say, brother, yer name Turnipseed?"

"Yes."

"Well, my man, you better put that funky bucket on yer ass, 'cuz Gunny Benson's been lookin' fer you all damned day."

"You don't say," I said. "Well, I suppose I ought to go say hello then?"

"Yeah, and you better say 'sir' and you better say both in a hurry. Let's go," he urged, as if to encourage me in the face of a grave and dangerous mission. He danced with clean strides through the clutter of the tent and out into the daylight at the other end, calling without turning back, "Let's go now, c'mon my boy, let's go."

"Okay, all right, already," I called as I followed.

He scurried through the tent ropes and wound deftly through the bunkers on the way to the company office. When I entered the tent, exhausted but inwardly laughing at Mountain Man's ebullience, I saw, sitting in a back corner, smoking a cigar as he reclined behind his desk, the same bald, long-scarred, and broken-nosed captain who had sent me off to guard duty. Another man, a short, middle-aged black man whose temples were just beginning to grey, wearing only his desert camouflage trousers and a brown T-shirt, was seated at the desk near the status board. I stepped up to the counter and announced myself.

"Is a Gunny Benson in? My name is Turnipseed, and it has just been brought to my attention that he has been looking for me."

The man at the desk glanced silently up from his work, then returned his attention to the papers strewn out across the desktop. Figuring that the gunny must be out, I turned to leave—

"You can just park your ass right here, Turnipseed," the man at the desk called out, head still bowed before his work. I stopped—uneasy, puzzled by his refusal to acknowledge my presence, by the silence that preceded, and now followed, his belated response.

I stood still and silent, looking into the miscellaneous mail on the countertop, noting the marks made on the letters, mostly, "Up North" or "Mishab" or "Medivac" until, after a seeming eternity, the gunny spoke again.

"So where you been, Turnipseed?"

"At the guard tents," I said, "and—and moving in."

"Uh, Morris," he called to Mountain Man smoothly, knowingly, like a parent, "what time did I send you over to the guard shack this mornin?"

"Zero-seven, Gunny." At which point the gunny gave a calculated look at his watch. My mind was reeling, trying to remember what time Sergeant Small had come into the tent that morning, groping for an exact time, for an excuse—it had been much later than seven, I was sure.

"Turnipseed," Gunny Benson asked, "I see you got a watch on. What's your watch say?"

"Yes, I have got one, haven't I," I sighed. This was a silly game, and an unfair one. "And it's been eight hours since you sent Morris to the guard shack. Is there something I can do for you?" It must have been around ten or so that Sergeant Small came into our tent. He must have waited to tell me of my reassignment, in order to let me rest after a night shift. My mind raced as I waited for him to reply.

"Yeah, there's something you can do for me," he said after pausing to consider his words carefully, "you can show the fuck up when I call for you, and you can stand there while I tell you what you can do for me. So, where you been—you still ain't answered my question . . . I know you ain't been at the guard shack all mornin,' 'cuz Morris here been runnin' his ass all over camp lookin' for ya. What's your story?"

"Would you like the unabridged or the *Reader's Digest* version?"

Morris winced.

"Come here, Turnipseed," the gunny beckoned. That he still hadn't looked up from his paperwork unnerved me. I walked around the counter, then moved toward the desk at which Benson sat. "Stop," he said, then turned to me. "Turnipseed? Why you wanna go and fuck me like this? Don't you know it's hard enough to be a fuckin' company gunny without having every little smart-ass try an' get his limp little dick up my ass?" he whispered. I laughed, lightly, as he leaned back in his chair.

"Sergeant Small just didn't tell me, didn't explain—"

"Sergeant Small got nothing to do with it, Turnipseed. I don't wanna hear no more excuses. Not to-fuckin'-day and not to-fuckin'-morrow. What you're gonna do for me now is find the duty driver, and tell him to get your ass down to Saudi Motors so you can get your license—and I better not see you again till you got one. Can you do that one little thing for me, Turnipseed?"

"Yeah, I can do it. Where's the duty driver?"

"Oh, he's probably fuckin' off somewhere where nobody can find him, just like everybody else today."

Morris, who had been standing to the side during the entire scene, stepped up. "Hey there, Turnipseed, I'll drive ya down there, brother. Got to go down that way anyhow."

Training lasted all of two hours. I learned to drive a semi with four easy classroom principles and fifteen minutes of behind-the-wheel training. I did not learn to back up. I also did not go up North to live with the guys from Minneapolis, but stayed in Jubayl, driving North to drop off trucks at Mishab and the surrounding ammunition supply points. I was assigned my first convoy early the following morning. On my first run I caught a rack mounted on the side of a guy's trailer. He was pretty pissed, but nothing critical had been damaged, so we chalked it up to inexperience.

I arrived back from tractor-trailer school shortly after sunset, and was surprised to find the tent was full. Seven or eight men, all Philly boys—all but one of whom were black, sitting in a half circle on the edge of two cots. Gunny Benson stood between them, hands in his pockets, hanging out with his boys. I crept through the tent flaps, camouflaged by the hanging laundry.

"Hey, brothers, who's the new dude?"

"Oh, that's Turnipseed," Morris answered. "I took his lost puppy ass in this mornin.' You was draggin' your sorry ass all *over* this compound, ain't that right, Turnipchew?"

"Yes," I said, still removing my flak jacket and H-harness, "that's right."

"Damn, we got ourselves a Poun' Puppy," exclaimed Hatch, who turned toward me. He lay on his cot, his broad shoulders propped by his elbows. His headphones hung around his neck, still playing. "Where you from, Turnipjew? You Jewish?"

"No, I'm Vegetable. And I'm from Minneapolis."

"Hey, Turnipseed," cried Morris, "don't that make you a *frozen* vegetable? Your ancestors come in a plastic bag like them peas and carrots and shit?"

"Hey, Mountain Man, you keep that beard goin' on, and maybe Turnipjuice can take your ass home with him. Go kill a bear or some crazy-ass shit like chipmunks. You got chipmunks in Minnesota?"

"Gophers," said Hatch, "motherfuckers got gophers, Bones."

"So tell me, brother Turnip," asked Ebbers, "how the fuck you live up there?"

"Well, you know, I sleep, eat food. Perambulate now and again. Read, chat on the phone once in a while. I mostly enjoy the time I spend relaxing and reading in the coffee shops."

"Coffee shops? Damn," said Hatch, "I knew you were a college boy. Good thing ol' Riley sitting cross from you is getting his master's degree at Temple. You two can translate each other for us—break it down."

"I suppose. Well, if you don't mind, I'd like to get some reading and writing done here. Sorry I can't be more fun."

"That's chill," said Hatch, "I'm in the middle of a book myself. Maybe Ebbers and Mountain Man here will zip it up for a while."

* * *

I laid out my things on my cot: journals, letters, fountain pen. At the foot of my bed lay my ALICE pack, with my flak jacket and H-harness draped over it, then came my gas mask, with my combat helmet topping the pile. To my left I had the portable bookshelf. All I lacked was a tawny port and a good smoke.

"Oh, and by the way," I asked, "do you guys mind if I smoke a pipe in here?"

"A pipe? No kidding? You some kind of professor or something?"

"Oh, he's absentminded all right, you just ask the gunny!" laughed Mountain Man.

"Yeah, you smoke that pipe," said Gunny Benson. "Out-fuckin'-side."

I unpacked my journals and books, but I couldn't read. I just sat and stared. I was exhausted, but awake. And my exhaustion was more than physical. I had long been trying to set myself up in conscious opposition to society, always comparing surface to some hidden reality—which I would discover in books and in philosophy. I no longer had the energy to process every perception as part of a syllogism. As for standing in opposition—my frontal assault on society wasn't going too well: the barrels of my guns were smoking and I was out of ammo. I was down to throwing paperback editions of Wittgenstein from my foxhole, wielding an empty fountain pen. But the enemy kept sending their hordes, sounding their trumpets as they stormed my Dead White barricades: whole divisions of Warner Brothers and Disney, Def Jam and Columbia, Wal-Mart and K-Mart and 7-11, Ray-Ban and Kodak, Nike and Gatorade, of Hatches and Farmers and Ebberses from privates to corporals to the Colonel's, chains of command and fast-food chains—it was just too much to overcome. I must have sat like that for an hour—but I wouldn't have known the difference if it had only been a minute.

"Hey, dude, we thought you got rigor mortis. You sit still like that all the time?"

"Sure, why not?" I felt compelled to be funny. "You know, I sit here and think Zen koans silently to myself: 'The One-Nut Vet. The Low or the High One?'"

"Damn, he's trippin', Eb. What you readin', Turnipseed?"

"Plato's *Republic*. Very un-Zen."

"You don't look like no Republican to me."

"Uh, Turnipchew?" called Mountain Man, "You ain't pullin' no sheep-wearin' wolf shit on me, are you? I coulda swore you had a damn Democratic draggin' ass this mornin'."

"Actually, the *Republic* is a philosophical dialogue, and though a naive reading may present it as a political tract (which, to a certain degree it *is*), it is really more a presentation, or parable, of the soul's journey through philosophy."

It's hard for me, now, to capture the tone of my rapport with the Dog Pound: it was natural, arch, warm, and funny. There was an immediate ease to our back-and-forth play.

"So . . . " began Ebbers, "so you really are the Professa. Well, Professa, what do you think of this shit? You think we should be over here dicking the dog for George Bush?"

"Actually," I replied, "I abjure sodomy."

"Hey, Mountain Man, did my man the Professa just say 'abjure sodomy' or did he say 'yer lobotomy'?"

Mountain Man stepped out into the aisle, brushing away some damp towels with great panache, "I believe he said, 'abjure sodomy,' my broth-ahhhh."

The two of them slapped a high five, while the rest of us laughed.

"Hey, Professa, later on you goin' to have to tell us what that meant."

"It means, 'I don't do no dogs.'"

"Uh-*huh*. Denyin' it already," said Morris. " Guess I'll zip up the sleeping bag extra tight, anyhow."

"Say, Morris?" I asked, "how'd you get the name Mountain Man?"

"Professor, you gotta see my man at Pearle Vision. Can't you see I got a mothafuckin' beard?"

Black Planet

Slowly, I began to live to a new mantra: "Fuck it, drive on." Or just "Fido."

It was an unavoidable force, like gravity or cigarettes at eighty-five cents a pack. Or Mountain Man's beard: he had shaving bumps so bad the Navy Corpsman had said, "Fuck it, grow a beard." Morris had to carry a permission chit everywhere he went.

And the rest of us had to drive on.

"My tires look a little bald" was answered by "Fido. Let's go."

Which was followed by "I only got two hours' sleep," and, "I guess you'll need to buy a full-fucking-carton of Camels at the truck stop, won't you." Fido. Fuck it, drive on.

After I took the front off that poor bastard's old Mercedes down at Saudi Motors, we drove on. Our convoy arrived home from our run to an ammunition supply point just as the sun was ready to plunge into the desert. Tired and dirty, my eyes lazy from passing over so many miles of unbroken black ribbon, I stepped into the tent. I was surprised by the festive atmosphere. I was immediately tired by it.

"Hey guys, what'd I miss?" I groaned.

"Just your mail, Professor," called out Morris, who quickly returned his attentions to Farmer and Ebbers, who were workin' out a rap in the tent-aisle.

Lying in a heap on my cot were: some letters, a care package from my stepfather's parents, and an "any-serviceperson" letter from some Michigan elementary school students. I opened the care package, then passed it over to Ebbers, then ran my Ka-Bar under the lid of the large manila envelope bulging with elementary school well-wishes. They sent me snapshots of their Thanksgiving pageant, and dozens of letters—scrawled as-neatly-as-possible—including one from Becky:

> *Dear Soldier I wish you were safe. from Becky B.*

And another from Eric:

> *I hope you don't get shot*
> *By Iraq cause some*
> *People shoot cause people*
> *Shoot all soldier*
> *To the soldier*
> *I like you*
> *Eric S.*

I smoked an entire cigarette trying to parse the first-grade intentions of Eric's haiku. Also in the mail were a letter from my mother—too thin—and the *New Republic*'s "Race on Campus" special issue. Nothing from Sarah. Mark had written a week earlier to tell me that an entire day of classes had been cancelled at the University for "sensitivity training." In one of the *New Republic* pieces, a Yale Law School professor wondered, "Why should classes be cancelled when students could better express their determination to fight racism by giving up something that really mattered to them, like a weekend?" Like a life. I imagined fighting a war on that basis: weekdays only, with keggers and an afterbar at the Iraqis' place. Saddam and Powell taking turns spinning. Then back to the trenches on Monday.

I looked up at the guys screwing around in the tent. "Say, did you guys know that it's Black History Month?"

"It's *what?!*" asked Ebbers. "Shit, Professa, *every* month's Black History Month."

"Yeah," said Hatch, "ain't nobody got to tell the Pound. You know, I think you have to come hang with the Pound in Philly, Professor. Show you what it means to be a brother. We might even get your ass laid."

"Hey, Professor," asked Mountain Man, "you ever do it with a sister?"

"Ahhh . . . " I stumbled, irony and surprise tripping over each other on my tongue. "No."

"That's cool. You come to Philly, and we'll hook you up."

Bones sat up about a half-inch in his cot, looking down his wide, round nose at me. "You ain't afraid of that, are you there, Punkin-strudel? I bet you think you're gonna catch herpes or somethin', huh?"

"Bones?!" cried Mountain Man, "What're you talkin' bout—you never been laid in your whole damn life. I know *you* afraid of the sisters. Leave my brother the Professor alone and go dream about a big ol' booty for your own self."

"Yeah, that's okay, Mountain Man, you just keep my big ol' gorilla butt in line for the white man. That's right, you just go ahead—I'll see you later, too."

"Hey, Professor," called Hatch, "you don't mind Bonesie, now. He looks dangerous, but inside, he's soft as a teddy bear, ain't that right, Bonesie? He's just a wrestling coach—you know, like, he ain't thinkin' 'bout no booty. Oh no."

Bones grinned ridiculously. And so I spent my evenings with the Dog Pound. Bones stealing my journals, then throwing them back on my rack—failing to find the incendiary anti-black or anti-Bones entries; Ebbers and I breakin' it down—always comical; Hatch and I talking about our lives outside the war. Though I was no longer spending as much time with Thoreau and Wittgenstein, I was laughing—and at the time, a stroke of good humor was the best stroke of luck I could have happened upon.

Most of the time, however, I drove. Then slept. Then drove. Then slept. Always the sleeping.

I woke, in the buttery, sixty-watt light of midnight, to the sound of Ebbers and Farmer messin' with each other:

"Hey, Ebbers, was that your motha I saw out the truck stop yesterday? Hollerin' 'Blow-jobs fifty cent, round the world for a dollar'?"

"Yeah, Farmer, but she wasn't gettin' no business 'cause your mama doin' it for two bits at the truck stop just before. She suckin' the sheets up dudes' ass, brother."

"Of course," I called out, "ain't neither one of 'em makin' a livin' wage, 'cause the two of you takin' all the business with that booty you been givin' away for free just outside the gate."

"Professa? How come your mama didn't swallow when I asked her?" cried Ebbers.

Farmer snapped Ebbers in the ass with his towel, "Damn, Eb—Professa's mama didn't swallow for you?"

The two of them left for the showers.

Meanwhile, I squinted out at the Rat digging around for loot stored beneath his cot. I somehow worked up the energy to blink. I watched Riley write an entire letter while Hatch lay on his cot, silently listening to his Walkman. Bones, Flowers, Simkins, and Luke were out on a run.

Ebbers surprised me on his return. "You learnin' fast, Professa. You sure you don't wanna be a black man?"

"Professor's lookin' to become black?" asked Mountain Man, standing between the tentflaps. "Crazy. Well, you goin' to have to wait till after this run, Professor. And you, too, Rat, I know your devious little ass wants to be black. Hatch and Riley, you gotta go with the Rat and Professor."

Fifteen minutes later, the four of us were sitting on our packs outside the dispatch warehouse down at the port, our rifles resting across our laps. We were waiting for more trucks to come in from their runs. We waited a little longer, and one of the dispatch sergeants yelled down from his roost, "Hey gentlemen, you have to go down to Saudi Motors to check out some trucks. The convoy whose trucks you're supposed to get ain't gonna be in for another hour or two."

It was a peaceful ride through the port area, and we arrived back at the warehouse just past one in the morning. The trucks checked out okay, but they didn't have any loading straps, so Hatch and I walked in through the Ali Baba garage doors, two stories high, and called up to the dispatch office.

"Yo! You got some straps up there?" asked Hatch.

One of the dispatchers peeked over a railing at us, a cup of coffee steaming in his hand.

"Well, gentlemen, I think there are some in that big box over there by the hatch, right next to the picnic tables. If there ain't none in there, I guess you're just SOL till that run gets back from Mishab."

Shit out of luck. "Uh-huh," I said, "and you wouldn't happen to have any more coffee up there, would you?"

His head disappeared for a second, then bobbed back out above the railing.

"No, I guess we don't have any coffee. I mean, just enough for us," he said. "We gotta stay up all night, you know."

"Thank you very little."

"Yeah, you bet."

The Rat and Riley had already ransacked the box, and had only come up with a dozen straps, about enough for one and a half trucks, depending on the load. Maybe two. Most times we liked to have at least eight straps on a truck.

"Hey, Professa," asked the Rat, "whadda you say you an' me go on a little reconnaissance mission?"

"What do you mean?"

"I mean the *Army* don't drive all its trucks. And it don't watch 'em at night, either."

"I imagine we'll have to requisition some straps then, won't we?"

"Good ol' Marine Corps Supply," he chuckled. The Rat was a footpad and mercenary of minderbendering proportions.

The Rat and I jumped into a five-ton, then drove the half-mile across the port to the Army lot, where, sure as hell, not a single soul stood guard. The Rat killed the headlights, then rolled the truck slowly onto the Army lot, parking it between two of their tractor-trailers, U.S. military issue, no less. Mag-Lites at the ready, we scurried, hunched over, between the Army trucks. In all, we scammed more than a dozen straps.

Our run that evening was to a warehouse on the outskirts of Jubayl. This place was an insane carnival of U.S. commercialism and over-the-top excess, not to mention a testament to corporate opportunism: they had pallets of Frisbees, Nerf balls, every variety of Wrigley's, Pepsi, Miller Sharps non-alcoholic beer, Snickers, Hallmark cards, Chunky Soup, Slim Jims. It was like a fucking 7-11 distribution center. We were there to pick up single-serving boxes of Kellogg's cereals: two tractor-trailers' worth, with two more tractor-trailers loaded with cartons of nonperishable milk.

Somehow, the Rat already knew the staff sergeant in charge of the warehouse. It was like he had a little black book. I would later find the Rat in possession not only of whiskey (strictly forbidden), but, after we'd moved to tents in the desert, a portable generator, a nineteen-inch color television, a VCR, and a stack of porn flicks. He was a North Philly Milo: when he managed to acquire a new shipment of suede desert boots, much cooler than the shiny black jungle boots, he only charged me twenty-five bucks a pair, and if I remember correctly, he even threw in a set of desert camouflage fatigues.

Sleeping was all. And when I slept, I slept hard. Then there was waking. Waking seemed more like reincarnation than morning. Of course, more often than not, it wasn't morning when I awoke. Instead, the light of dangling bulbs; slow swinging shadows. The slap of plastic shower shoes against a puddle outside the tent.

I blinked my way into consciousness. Around me: empty cots with rumpled sleeping bags, crusty socks dangling from cot frames, and letters, their once-crisp corners crumpled and dirty from much and long handling. Music: Public Enemy, but played softly. A shout in the distance. Listening to the music, lying or sitting on their cots were Hatch,

Bones, and Riley. As I sat up and lit a cigarette, Ebbers walked in and asked, "Say Professa, you 'fraid of a Black Planet?"

Heads rose behind him, all eyes trained on me. Would I diss him? Fumble socially and say the offending word? Or swing with it, judo-like, and earn laughter—a now familiar routine.

"Only if you runnin' it, Ebbers."

Laughter. Ebbers eyes roll and Hatch, behind him, looks on at me shaking his head, smiling.

"Damn, Professa, why you wanna go an' do me like that?"

"Cuz I don't know if you're fuckin' with me or asking a serious question."

"Hey, Professor," Hatch broke in, "Whadda you mean it ain't serious? You don't think the brothers should get some? Now, I ain't whinin'—I'm just saying, you know, it's *hard* to be a black man, Professor."

"So okay, it's serious—how you going to get a Black Planet?"

"Me?" yelled Ebbers, grabbing his dick. "I'm just going to get me some!"

We all laughed, but the laughter died down quickly.

"Very funny, Eb. But do you think that some asshole grabbin' his dick on the city bus is goin to make it *easier?*"

"No dick-grabbin'?" yelped Ebbers. "Professa, you sayin' you don't wanna grab my dick no more? Serious, now—I'm gonna procreate and recreate so's I can just plain *create* me a Black Planet."

"Yeah, what're you tryin' to say, there, Mr. Nietzschenstrudel?" asked Bones.

"I'm sayin' what Socrates was sayin' in Book One of the *Republic:* That if a man does injustice he harms himself as much as anyone else; that he damages his soul."

"Now, I know you really be diggin' that dude, Professa, but you know, he ain't white like all the people tryin' to keep us down say he was."

"What?"

"You heard me, Professa: Socrates was a *Brotha.*"

"I saw a picture once, man, dude look like James Earl motherfuckin' Jones."

"Yeah, frien' of mine showed me a quote from Aristotle saying 'Socrates is black.'"

"Actually, that's from the *Metaphysics*. The section on predication. It also says that Socrates was white. And he doesn't look like James Earl Jones, he looks like Richard Dreyfuss."

"Okay, so even if they're white, they stole the *ideas* from the Africans. You gonna deny *that*, Professa?"

"You mean the Egyptians?"

"Yeah, and the mothafuckin' Ethiopians where the Egyptians stole it."

"Actually, there is no evidence that Socrates ever went to Egypt. Plato may have gone, but his primary influences were thought to be the Pythagoreans in Italy and, manifestly, Socrates. Other Greek thinkers certainly went to Egypt: Herodotus, Solon, and Thales, I think, but it is hard to say what and whether Egyptian thought influenced them. Besides which, the Egyptians weren't really 'black.'"

All hell broke loose.

"Professor, you in *college?* I don't think so, 'cause I got to school your ass."

"Professa, you tryin' to say the DJ's lyin' to our dumb black asses? 'Cause I know you ain't. I just don't know what it is you tryin' to say."

"Okay, fine, so they were black. Tan. Whatever. I can't say." I was scrambling. What to say? What could I say? Fuck it, when you can't say, *ask.* "Let me ask you this . . . ?"

"Strudelocrates, I know you ain't gonna say nothin' stupid again," said Bones.

"What if, let's say, the Egyptians *did* invent axiomatic geometry, mathematical astronomy, physics and philosophy . . . and the Greeks *did* steal it. Wouldn't it then be incumbent upon blacks to regain their heritage by studying physics, mathematics and philosophy?"

The air in the tent was, well, still. Bones was looking at me with an intensity that suggested that, perhaps, I had a *secret* journal in which I

was keeping my thoughts on the black man. Ebbers was downright per-
plexed. Hatch and Riley were both chewing the inside of their lips in
thought.

"Well, maybe, Professor," said Hatch, "but you know, it ain't like any-
body make it easy for us to study that shit . . . You know, nobody in my
school gave a shit 'bout philosophy. What's up with that?"

"Actually, very few people anywhere give a shit 'bout philosophy. But
that hasn't stopped philosophers from thinking. You see me lookin'
around the fuckin' camp, 'Hey Gunny Benson, you mind if I read a little
Plato this mornin' 'fore I go out on this run?'"

Ebbers puffed out his chest, and reached around to scratch his ass,
bellowing like Benson, "Turnipseed, you tryin' to shove that Play-Doh in
my ass again?"

"Ha-ha, very funny, Punkinstrudel," said Bones. "You tryin' to make a
joke, but I can see right through you. And don't think I can't."

"Actually, Bones ——"

"ACTUALLY." The entire tent mocked a nasal white-man's voice.

"Actually," I said, "Plato might just dig you, Bones. Did you know that
the ancient Greek word for 'friend' or 'close family member' was
oikeion—which literally meant 'homey'?"

We had a great thing going, the Pound and me. We'd drag-ass in from
our shifts out on the road, then trade insults and insights from Plato and
Public Enemy. I loved these moments but there were precious few of
them. We were hardly ever around the tent: always out driving. We were
some drivin' motherfuckers.

The air was still chilly and crisp when I arrived at the dispatch office before dawn, the lights sparkling all through Camp Shepard and
the port area. Our trucks sat waiting for us, headlights burning
through the fog, engines rumbling the soft snore of idleness. We made
a quick walk-around inspection to see if the previous driver had
missed anything, or been crazy enough to drive an unsafe tractor-
trailer. We were usually as tired, or crazy, or blind as the previous

driver. Then we drove down to the loading docks, jockeying for last place and the longest nap.

After being loaded with pallets of 155 mm artillery shells, we drove slowly back through the camps, rolling through the mists to the fuel dump just inside the gates of the port area. Dozens of red and yellow brake and tractor lights swept and circled ahead of us like fireflies.

At the refueling station, a man in olive-drab overalls three sizes too big shouted, "UNIT?"

"SIXTH MOTOR TRANSPORT BATTALION," I replied. Our cries hardly added to the cacophony produced by the rumble of diesel engines, the low cry of air brakes and slow grinding of transmissions, the whir of fuel pumps and generators.

"AWRIGHT," he said, pointing to a fuel line lying in the sand at road's edge. After killing the engine, I stepped down out of the cab and walked round to it, wrestling the heavy canvas hose over to my first tank, mounted above the rear wheels of the tractor. The attendant stood behind me, taking down numbers from the clicking pump, which was buried far down into the ground, sticking out just enough to expose the gauges.

Makeshift auxiliary tanks had been welded to the rear of our cabs, and I stepped up to mine, raised the fuel hose chest-high to fix it in the tank, then began pumping.

"HEY, YOU UP THERE! YOU'RE GETTING FUEL EVERYWHERE! HEY!"

I stopped pumping, looking around for the commotion.

"YEAH, *YOU*, ASSHOLE!"

I jumped down from my truck, without bringing the hose, then yanked the hose back like a flycaster, scattering the men behind me. Fuel was spraying from a bad weld down one edge of the auxiliary tank, like a diesel sprinkler. Better yet, it was spraying straight toward the rear, all over my artillery shells.

"Hey, man, why don't you get up there and cap that thing," said the attendant.

I climbed up the back of my truck, arching my body to stay behind the spray, and screwed the cap back on the tank. From there, I could see that everyone at the fuel dump was staring at me. Oshkosh-B'Gosh was my convoy commander again, and he was making his way toward my truck, slowly. He looked at me, lifting his hand into the spray of diesel, as if checking a shower.

"Ah, it's just a light stream," he said. "You'll have enough to make it to Mishab on your main tank, anyway."

"Is *that* what you're concerned with?" I asked. "What about, you know, *fire?*"

"Fire? With diesel? I could put a cigarette out in that stuff. Want me to show you?"

"No," I said, jumping down, "no thanks. I think I better take this thing back."

"Jeezus, kid, it's all right. No kidding. Wanna take my truck? I got the Mack, two clutches—you know how to drive it?"

I looked up at the flaccid streams of diesel, still twisting from the tank in golden ribbons toward their splash upon the pallets of shells. *Two clutches.*

"I'll be all right," I said, "just make sure someone keeps an eye on my back side, okay?"

"Okay!" he said, "Let's roll."

The sun was coming up over the Gulf just as our four-truck convoy pulled out the front gate. We had heavy traffic all the way out to the Abu Hadriyah Highway, and I half-felt like driving maniacally so that I could get pulled over by the road marshals. If I was lucky enough to get condemned to the side of the highway, I might be able to finish Whitman's *Democratic Vistas.*

As it turned out, the road marshals were the only ones who *didn't* try to pull me over. As the morning wore on, I developed a kind of gallows braggadocio. Some guys in a German water tanker pulled up next to me, waving frantically.

"Ach, ach, you got problem!"

I waved back, "Yeah, I got problems. We've all got 'em."

"No, no, you gotta leak back there! Number-one problem!"

"No, I'll take care of that at Mishab. Number two, too."

"YOU GOT FUEL LEAK!"

"Oh, that! You know the Corps, 'Fuck it, drive on.'"

They looked at each other, then floored it to clear my general vicinity. After a while, my cravings got me believing the bit about cigarettes and diesel. I was half-finished with my first smoke of the run when some Brits pulled up. I tipped the cherry out the window to clear an ash (trusting—*hoping*, that it was true that I could put the thing out in diesel), when a thick-mouthed A-driver called to me,

"'Ay, 'ay, ya know ya got fewel leekin' all ovuh ya lode?"

I smiled at him, then tossed the lit remainder of my cigarette out the window, where it disintigrated in a shower of sparks, "Yeah, you can put a cigarette out in that!"

"Shit you can, lad. You're bloody nuts!"

"Bloody nuts? A bloody good bloody thing, I say!"

A hissing sound rose from the rear of the cab. I flashed my headlights nervously, despairing that none of the three trucks ahead of me would notice my signal in the bright daylight. I gave up and angled for the narrow shoulder. I was just crunching to a standstill when a great *Thump-wump* echoed through the cab, sending me diving out the door with my ALICE pack and flak jacket.

Nothing happened. No smoke. It could be a flat. I crouched around the perimeter of my truck, and couldn't find a flat. Better than Whitman: I had a mystery. I looked underneath the truck. I checked the hoses. The load straps. I looked for broken supports beneath the trailer. Then I noticed that the fuel was no longer leaking. There was a long crease in the metal tank, with paint peeling along its ridges: the tank had emptied in such a way that it created a vacuum, and when enough fuel escaped, air replaced it and popped the tank back into shape.

My convoy was long gone.

* * *

I caught up with the rest of my convoy up at Ammunition Supply Point 3, a labyrinth cut out of sand in which acres of ammo were stored like food in an ant colony. Though I arrived two and a half hours later, I was only a half-dozen trucks behind the rest of my convoy. Still, our line stretched out into the road beyond the ASP. It looked like a long wait.

I removed my helmet, popped the clutch into first, cut the engine, and stretched out my legs. After taking a long drink of warm, chlorinated water mixed with half a packet of Taster's Choice left over from an MRE, I reached for my Whitman and a cigarette. Uncle Walter barely had a chance to yawp before a storm cloud appeared beyond my driver's-side window. With a warrant officer at its center.

"Goddammit! Goddammit! Goddammit! Are you tryin' to blow us back to Adam and Eve?"

He jumped up to my running board, poking his leathery face and beady brown eyes into the cab.

"Put that fuckin' thing out. Now! Now! Now!" he screamed, reaching half-assedly for the offending smoke. I looked at him, one brow raised, then quietly ashed it in its tray. I sighed with bemused fascination as I twisted out the cherry.

"Do you know, Marine, that you are smoking in an ammunition dump. You are a short fuse on a dangerous mission. CHRISSAKE: A GODDAM AMMO DUMP, BOY!"

"Actually," I began.

"ACTUALLY? What's your name, boy?"

"Joel. And strictly speaking, I'm not *in* the ammo dump."

"Sir! What's your rank, Joel?"

"Lance corporal."

"Sir, Sir, Sir! I'm a goddam officer, for Chrissake!"

"Whatever."

He stuck his face right up into mine, so that my glasses fogged with halitosis burn, "Listen, Marine," he said, "I want to impress upon you that this is no joking matter. This is a goddam serious-ass war we're fighting here. I can see you think it's funny. Well it's not, and I'm serious as a heart attack. If I see you smoking again, I'm gonna yank your tractor-trailer license so fast you're gonna . . . you're gonna . . . it's gonna feel like the road got yanked from beneath your wheels, if I can meta-goddam-phorically state my case. You understand me?"

I looked at him, quite non-metaphorically stunned. "Yes. *Sir.*"

In the end, "Fido" did not imply a lazy or haphazard approach, nor the fake pragmatism of the shitbird, but rather a kind of tough-guy jazz, an at-hand improvisation that recognized "Fuck it—you're a Marine—drive on," was a better alternative to the tragic and the unexpected than giving up or giving in, and the only way to survive the tragic until it stretched out to the comic.

"Hey, Bonesie, fuckin' with the Professor again?" Hatch called out as he sauntered into the tent, Ebbers, Farmer, Luke, and Riley filing in behind him. The sunlit dust was still dancing wildly from the motion of their fresh-flung flak jackets, helmets, rifles, gas masks, and ALICE packs when outside the tent Gunny Benson hollered, "Formation!"

"Shit, Gunny, cool it a second, I got to go dukey."

The gunny poked his bald head inside the tent, "Ebbers, don't be givin' me any of that shit. You got fifteen minutes."

Half an hour later, we were all standing in formation, along with the dozen or so other Bravo Company guys who weren't out on runs.

"Okay, listen up! I'm gonna save y'all some time for letters, so I'm only gonna say this once. Seems we got some hygiene problems with you animals:

"—Start changin' your skivvies and brushin' your teeth, the fuckin' corpsman be passin' out when y'all go to medical.

"—Stop pissin' outside your tent. Ain't nobody told you not to shit where you eat?"

"Hell, we don' eat in there, Gunny."

"I got you on ignore, Ebbers. Now, I got some real nice word to pass to y'all. Ya got to go an' get another anthrax shot."

"I ain't got the first one yet."

"Well, you just better ask for two, then, huh? You gentlemen got to get these things. I got mine an' I ain't dead yet."

We looked at each other: "Dude, you a crusty old Vietnam vet Marine. Ain't nothin' gonna kill your old leather ass."

Gunny Benson didn't wait for us to deliberate. "Okay, I understand Professor Turnipseed here's got some word to pass, ain't that right, Turnipseed?"

"I'm sorry, Gunny, but did I miss something?"

"Well, my boys here been tellin' me you been schoolin' 'em. I feel like I'm bein' left out of the educational process. So why don't you just come on up here an' pass some educational word for the rest of us?"

Motherfucker. I was being put up to it.

"C'mon Professa, get some goin' on."

Hesitantly, I broke ranks, taking a spot before Gunny Benson in front of the formation.

"Well, all right, here's some word for you guys," I said, looking out at the twenty or so men assembled before me. "It is, appropriately enough, related to our discussion the other night in the Pound: 'Men esteem truth remote, in the outskirts of the system, behind the last star, before Adam and after the last man. But. . . . The universe constantly and obediently answers to our conceptions; whether we travel fast or slow, the track is laid for us.' Henry Thoreau."

"Uh, Professa, I'm afraid you're gonna have to break it down for us," called Ebbers.

"Awright," I said, pausing for a moment to gather myself, my persona, then broke it down in the worst rap. Ever.

> What my man with the funky trou'
> tryin' to say to y'all

is "Don't go lookin' down the block
for what you need to rock,
cuz there's nothin' there
to help you cure ya cares.
An every thing that got you illin'
You make yo'self while you is chillin'—
So if you don't trust ya'self today,
ya ain't gonna tomorrow: no-way
— and not the next day neithuh.
You got to know ya'self,
Use ya own wisdom's welf,
and cure ya own self of ya' fevuh."

Gunny Benson, smiling quizzically, turned toward the formation. "What the fuck'd you do to ol' Turnipseed here, gentlemen? You have truly fucked with his head."

"*Nawwwwwww,* Gunny. He just picked that shit up his own self," answered Mountain Man. "Ain't that right, Professor?"

I grinned and replied: "Word."

Snow Angels

THE GROUND WAR STARTED, but with the return of the SCUD alarms excepted, we didn't notice. For several weeks, Saddam had his SCUD launchers hanging low, under cover of desert camouflage and out of radar mode. Now we could sense the end of the war with each distant thundering of the Patriot missile batteries as Saddam let loose with a desperate finale. We had no idea how it would end, but rumors flew: we'd go all the way to Baghdad, we'd stick Saddam's head on a pike, Marines would storm the beaches of Kuwait in the first amphibious assault since World War II. Of course, the devastations also became increasingly apparent: black skies at midday, trucks and equipment littered all over the desert, and oil slicks stretching all along the Gulf.

In our case, any ending would be a tired one, as all we knew for sure was that we would keep driving. Or, with increasing frequency as we continued to lay waste to the tractor-trailer population of Saudi Arabia, not driving: I had one truck break down just after getting loaded at the dock. Since we couldn't leave a loaded truck, I had to stand guard on a truck stalled less than fifty feet from the fence between the port warehouses and our tent camp. I could smell the chow hall on the breeze while I ate my barbecued-beef MRE.

Hatch was nice enough to come by with my mail. I felt like I was tree-sitting without an audience. After preparing my pipe for a smoke, I opened a letter from Mary, my buddy Mark's wife, but more importantly, Sarah's older sister. She wrote movingly of watching CNN in the student union, and Mark's "Herzog" phase: writing letters to Congress, friends, but not yet to the Queen of England. She wrote nothing of Sarah.

* * *

And this absence made her presence stronger. Sitting alone, in the midday sun, parked in a dead truck near the port warehouses, I thought of our last moments together.

We'd intended to head for a park, to go sledding, but instead of a park we found ourselves at the University. It had begun snowing again, a fitful snow following a harsh and bitter Christmas. We parked just off campus and headed for Northrup Mall, kicking up snowbursts with our steps and gazing around us in wonder: the trees glistened and the snow danced beneath the streetlights. The buildings sat serenely by, partially masked by flurry and shadow. The world went on quietly, existing for our pleasure—an active partner to our unfolding frolic. Our steps lightened to a skip, then a near-jog, as we made our way down the center of the broad, empty streets paved with a gleaming surface of snow.

We arrived on the mall, a long open rectangle punctuated by tall trees as old or older than the University itself. Surrounding it, well-lit columns stood forward from the shadows in which the buildings hid, dozens of columns, standing down each row and at either end, chests sticking out in Grecian glory. Alone under the bright lights framing the mall, our voices echoed into the night, our screams and laughter barely muffled by the snow.

"I want to make angels," protested Sarah, pirouetting through calf-deep snow, sending it showering in a cloud about her legs. As I watched her land, her face shimmering and surrounded by a halo of light and snow, a shock of pain ran through me. A long-distant recognition— desire. I had desired before, but it had been a long time. Too much pain. I was numbed and stood still, staring as Sarah danced through the air in another pirouette.

"Well, *are* we going to make angels, or *aren't* we?" asked Sarah.

Without hesitation, I plopped down on my back, wagging my arms and legs in the snow and calling out to the boughs and stars above me, "Men lie on their backs, talking about the fall of man, without making the effort to get up!—And why the hell not? They're making angels!"

Sarah joined me, splashing snow up into the air. It rained down in cold sprinkles upon my face: kisses from snow angels.

Being Bombed

BEING BOMBED IS BORING. It was thrilling, at first, to have the SCUDS start falling: when the sky flashed and the desert rumbled; when I and the other frightened Marines scattered like roaches from our tents, wearing nothing but gas masks and dog tags and underwear. Outtakes from our first days of war splashed back into our senses: the mad scramble of five SCUD alarms our first night in Saudi Arabia—one of the missiles scaring us senseless by exploding right near the acres of 155-millimeter shells we'd soon be trucking to the front lines; the tumble of sandbags in half-assed bunkers; Robin twitching on his cot from the side effects of the nerve gas pills.

Now the sky was screaming again.

By the second or third night of the war, the thrill of being awakened two or three or four times turned to something more like annoyance. Imagine shuffling to the portable toilet in your flip-flops and gas mask, closing the door, taking your seat, then hearing the low grumbling whine of the first siren. Then all the ones that followed, and they were everywhere—even the civilian mosques were outfitted with alarms—and now they're all sounding at once. You're tired. You've heard sirens all night long. So do you get up and run? No, you light a cigarette there in your stinking fiberglass outhouse and hope the shrapnel will bounce off the walls.

After a couple weeks of this, if the sirens came on while I was asleep, I didn't even bother to get out of my cot. I just drew my flak jacket over my chest, pulled on my helmet and cradled my gas mask like a teddy bear. The first night I declined the invitation of the sirens, Schuyler and Bergman flipped my cot and dragged me out of the tent by the legs. My desperate act of laziness was noted by others, however, and the next time the alarm sounded, while most people scrambled for shelter, I saw Blegen smoking silently on his cot. Heinemann was sitting on his, shuffling a deck of cards.

"What're odds one of these things actually hits?" he asked.

"Long," I said.

"Well, Turnip, I'll give you 5 to 1 if you guess the number of attacks tonight and 10 to 1 if you guess how many get taken out by the Patriots—100 to 1 if you tell me where they strike if we miss."

So we became the bookies of our own deaths. I didn't feel grim enough to bet, but Blegen did, laying down five bucks on five attacks. He didn't play the trifecta, though, and leaned back on his cot to sleep through the rest of the alarm. So did I: When you rarely got more than four or five hours' sleep, you didn't want to run yourself ragged for the long odds of a SCUD strike.

When the air war got decently underway and the A-10s went SCUD hunting, we enjoyed a several-week respite. But as soon as we crossed the berms, Saddam was back at it with a fury. I was in the middle of writing an article for my college newspaper, *The Minnesota Daily*, when the déjà vu'd. As I was describing the beauty of the desert, the first alarm came, and the surprise roused me from my cot and out to a bunker. Attack No. 2 occurred just two sentences into Paragraph 8, Attack 3 in Paragraph 10. I wanted to make the next mail drop at the Conex post office, so I stayed put. Ebbers and Mountain Man came in from the alarm, fuming.

"Motherfucker 'bout pissing me off!" said Ebbers. "How's a man supposed to get some sleep around here? Saddam don't cut this shit out, I'm a fuck him up myself."

"Stay in your cot," said Luke, echoing into the rubber of his gas mask, which he'd pulled over his face while he continued to maintain a fitful sleep.

"You crazy, Luke," said Ebbers, "You and the Professor gonna get your asses killed."

"You think a three foot pile of sandbags is going to protect you better than this tent, Eb?" asked Hatch. "Next one comes, I'm staying in my cot. I'm so tired I'm going to die, anyway—may as well accelerate the process."

When the alarms for that fourth SCUD started whirling, half the Pound ignored it.

The bomb exploded right overhead, and the concussive effect of the explosion knocked the wind out of us. Through some pure, adrenalin-charged order from our animal brain, we sped out to the shelter. No cognition involved. It wasn't until we saw one another, sitting in the bunker wearing fogged-up gas masks, that we were able to piece together the events: Alarm. Explosion. Shelter. Gas Masks. Weird, incomprehensible stares. After a few minutes' silence, we collectively shrugged, then went back to our tent.

Hatch turned on American Forces Radio to hear the news. There was no mention of our attack, just the tragic report from the Khobar barracks, where twenty-eight Army soldiers were killed by an Iraqi SCUD and a hundred more wounded—making WATER PURIFICATION SPECIALIST the most dangerous job in the Gulf. Why didn't they run for their bunkers? Maybe because they didn't have time. Or maybe because war is boring. Bombing is tedious. And during war's long drag, we all exhaust our inner resources.

Still, when the report ended and the evening's fifth SCUD alarm sounded, we ran like motherfuckers for the bunkers, tired brains and flak jackets and rifles—all just baggage on our strange trip.

Getting Lost

A ND THEN THE WAR WAS OVER. Six weeks of bombing and Tomahawk
missile attacks and artillery shelling. Done. We had hauled fifty-
seven ships' worth of 155 mm shells, plastic explosives, napalm, milk
boxes, cereal, tents, medical supplies, tanks, APCs, uniforms, Frisbees,
Coke and Pepsi, boots and batteries, and men from Al Jubayl to Al
Mishab, then to Kibrit and Al Khanjar. During the buildup in February
we had hauled fifteen days' worth of ammunition for the entire Marine
Corps in a total of 3,755 runs in only ten days. Of some 1,400 tractor-
trailers leased from Saudi civilians, nearly 600 were trashed, sitting on
the shoulder of the Abu Hadriyah Highway or the four-lane road
plowed through the desert from Mishab to Kibrit to Al Khanjar. We
may have been reservists, but we were also the Baghdad Express, and
from the time we arrived in Saudi Arabia until the war ended we had
collectively driven more than 10,000 round trips. If you counted a
round trip as the full, two-leg run from Al Jubayl to Al Khanjar and
back—a six-hundred-mile journey—that would put us over six million
miles, only half of which was driven on asphalt highway. We were exhausted. We had just moved more ammunition over a longer distance in
a shorter period of time than any other unit in the history of war.

Now we had to undo the whole thing.

We had to clear the port of Jubayl of all the ammunition so that the pull-
out could begin; so the ammunition could be surveyed and sold to the
Kuwaitis and Saudi Arabians. During the war, we had always driven in
convoys. Three or four trucks, depending on how many made it back

from Al Mishab. But when I showed up at the warehouse down at the port this time, they told me to take the lone truck idling outside.

"You're going up to ASP-3 by yourself today," said Robin, who hadn't left the port the entire war. "You need a map?" I must have driven up there a dozen times. "It's right off the Abu Hadriyah, but it's easy to miss. I think the guys said the turnoff was marked by some tires and a red flag or a Toyota or something."

I scrounged around for some load straps, then headed out to the port in my truck. The sun was just rising as I filled up at the fuel farm. The guys at the front gate waved me through without looking at my trip ticket, and I was on the road with another truck full of artillery shells.

I was driving past the on-ramps to the two-laners that went out to the airport and refineries. It was odd to drive alone, cruising the highway with a cigarette dangling from my lips and no other trucks on the road. The skies were filled with black smoke, 360 degrees on the horizon, dark like oncoming night. With the sun beating down on my truck, I felt like I was driving dead center in the middle of the Twilight Zone. I was lost. I had missed the exit to the Abu Hadriyah. The first exit I came to after figuring out I had blown it was a cloverleaf that went nowhere. Fifteen minutes later I came to another exit, and turned right heading north on a freshly paved two-laner. After hitting eighth gear I lit a cigarette, but hadn't even flicked the first ash from it when I slammed on the brakes. The road came to an end. Bam. The End. No more road—nothing but a pile of gravel in the sand. There were tire tracks leading off the end of the road, so I figured it was safe to drive on. I pulled slowly off the highway, then eased into second gear around the construction site. It was muddy, but I made it through—until I had to climb back onto the highway.

I was stuck.

I didn't even know how to back up the truck. When a Filipino driving a water tanker came rolling through the desert behind me, I felt simultaneously relieved and like a shithead. He parked his truck behind me, then jumped out of his cab.

"Hey, you stuck?"

"Yeah."

"I'll push, you drive out, okay?"

I put the truck in gear, then sat on the clutch. When I felt the tanker smash into my trailer, I let out the clutch and gave it hell. I was free. A quarter-mile up the highway I pulled off to the shoulder, waiting for the Filipino to come and give me directions. When I looked back, he'd vanished.

I drove back out to the highway I'd turned off, then headed east. I looked at the highway signs, which were marked in English and Arabic. So I could read them. But I couldn't really *read* them: a startlingly obvious fact when you're in a foreign desert is that a highway sign without a map is meaningless. I was going nowhere.

A SPIN-2 satellite image of the Jubayl area taken March 8, a week and a half after I had gotten lost, shows my embarrassment with an accuracy of 1.5 meters per pixel: Better than a map, even without the highway signs. Sadly, I lacked a satellite uplink and laptop in my truck. I was not only missing the art-directed, jump-cut, theme song war on television—I couldn't even find it in broad daylight. I looked through the dusty windshield and tried to figure out what I was going to do next. I decided to head back to Jubayl and try to retrace my steps.

I couldn't even find Jubayl. Instead, I drove all the way to the Gulf, stopping in traffic lights in a city that looked nothing like Jubayl. At best, I was cruising through the suburbs like an ammo-laden idiot. I ignored the stares of Saudis driving their Toyotas, looking back and forth between me and my 155 mm shells. I gave them a cursory nod, then exhaled a drag from my cigarette, like I was totally cool, on a secret mission or something. I ended up driving north along the coast, figuring I would find a switchback or frontage road to the Abu Hadriyah. Instead I ended up on a point jutting out into the Persian Gulf, parked in front of the gates of a Saudi Arabian Coast Guard station. About a dozen guys came flying out of the single-story office, waving their arms at me. They began screaming at me in Arabic.

I leaned out of my cab and asked, "Abu Hadriyah?"

All twelve of them pointed their arms out to the west, which was nothing but a stretch of sand and scrub-brush and the scraggliest-looking sheep I'd ever seen. They had wool hanging off them like kudzu.

"Look, guys, I'm lost," I said. "Do any of you speak English?"

They looked at each other, then a pair of them jogged back to the building. A guy wearing epaulets came out, speaking perfect English.

"I understand you are lost," he said. "For where are you looking?"

"The Abu Hadriyah Highway."

"It's directly west of here," he said, pointing as the others had done. "If you can turn your vehicle around, I'll let you follow me back to the highway."

The road I was on led straight out into the Gulf along a causeway. The lot at the Coast Guard station wasn't big enough to turn a donut in a Buick. I pulled out into the sand. I got stuck. The Saudi Coast Guard men returned from the office carrying shovels, like this was a normal deal, no different than Minnesotans getting out from under a blizzard, buddies from the neighborhood digging a forty-ton semi loaded with ammo out of the sand. While I was looking at a map with the officer, one of the guys jumped into my truck. He was lighting up the tires in the sand, spraying his pals with grit and smoke. I thought the engine was going to explode. Then the guy rocketed forward and everybody cheered like he was Evel Knievel jumping the fountains at Caesar's Palace.

I wound up spending the night in the desert, stuck for a third time. This time I had buried my entire semi up to the cab in sand, on the road leading from the Abu Hadriyah to the ammo supply point. I found the exit from the highway all right, exactly as Robin had described it, complete with totaled Camry next to a stack of tires bearing a red flag in the center. It was on the unimproved road to the ASP that I screwed myself.

I was approaching a crew of Americans with a front-end loader and a tracked bulldozer filling a washed-out crater in the middle of the road. The road wasn't wide enough for me to pass them, I had already gotten stuck in the mud once, and it had begun raining; so I figured I'd just gun it and ride the edge of the road past the engineers in the mud-hole. I shifted down to fourth, then third—then the engine seized and I just about went through the windshield. The engineers were looking at me like they'd just dosed themselves with the morphine kits from their gas-mask pouches.

I jumped out of the truck to see how things looked. Bad. I had plowed up a berm in front of my truck, and the sand was packed all the way up to the cab.

"Hey, dude," one of the operators called out, "lemme give you a hand." He swung his bulldozer around on its tracks, then pushed the berm away from the front of my truck. Then he swung around again and backed up to the cab. He walked right over the back of the bulldozer and tossed down the first few links of a chain. At the end of the chain was an S-hook the size of a boot, the links as big as my fist. I kicked away enough sand to hook the chain onto the frame, then jumped into the cab. The engineer turned around to look at me, then gave a thumbs-up as he rolled forward. When the frame of the semi began creaking, I put the pedal to the floor, but except for the frame and the bumper, the truck didn't move an inch.

"Wow, dude, you really parked this sonofabitch, didn't you?"

"Guess so," I said.

"Well, we gotta be heading back to camp. We'll tell someone you're here."

"Stuck like a motherfucker," said the other guy, shaking his head.

As I watched the crew roll away into the sunset, I noticed that I had lost my fountain pen and my pipe. It was pouring. I stepped out to look around my truck, but couldn't find them after several walk-arounds and gave up. I was shivering miserably when I got back into the cab. The whole run was only supposed to take a few hours and I had forgotten to bring my parka. I had forgotten to bring an MRE. I didn't even have water with me. I looked down at my MOPP gear in its brown plastic bag and considered ripping them open to wear as pajamas, but then decided against it. I crawled up into the bunk behind the cab and crashed.

And not till we are completely lost, or turned round—for a man needs only to be turned round once with his eyes shut in this world to be lost—do we appreciate the vastness and strangeness of nature. Every man has to learn the points of compass again as often as he awakes, whether from sleep or any abstraction. Not till we are lost, in other words not till we have lost the world, do we begin to find ourselves, and realize where we are and the infinite extent of our relations.

Walden, 8:2

Thoreau's *Walden* was, during these years, my scripture. I numbered the paragraphs, chapter by chapter, of my Modern Library edition. This book was my compass; it was my *Realometer*. No matter what other book was with me, *Walden* was sure to be near at hand as well.

As I passed the night in my truck, alone in the middle of the Arabian desert, I tried to test my life by this scripture. I tried, but could not. As I flipped through the pages, I began to read this as an extraordinarily sad, lonely, almost desperate book. I began to mourn it.

"Hey," a voice cried out. "Hey, you in there. You stuck or something?"

I looked down over the driver's seat at the face peering in the window.

"No, I'm camping. You the roadmaster?"

"No, I'm with the Sixth Motor Transport Battalion. Who are you?"

"Turnipseed. I'm in Bravo Company. Go tell the roadmaster I'm stuck up to my ass out here, would ya?"

"Yeah, I'll tell the dispatchers when I get back to Mishab. Jesus, you really stuck this thing, didn't you?"

"Sure did."

"Well, good luck, buddy."

It went on like this all night. Every half hour someone would come by, asking me if I was stuck. I was smoking a cigarette and still reading *Walden* when the first Philly boy showed up.

"Hey, 'zat you, Professa?"

"Yeah, it's me, Farmer. I'm stuck."

"Ain't that the fuckin' shit. Gunny Benson know you're out here?"

"Got me. Roadmaster's been told about a dozen times, though."

"Damn, man. You stuck up to your ass. And it's a cold motherfucker tonight. You need a parka, Professa?"

"Farmer, you're a legend if you've got an extra parka."

"I ain't got an extra one, but let me give you mine. You need food or water or something?"

"Yeah, an MRE would be great. Water, too."

"I'm hookin' you up, ain't I, Professa?"

"Fuckin' A, Farmer."

"Okay, now, I gotta get back to Jubayl. I'll tell Gunny and the Mountain Man. We'll have you outta here in no time. 'Night, Professa."

The parka was still warm from Farmer's body.

> *I say, beware of all enterprises that require new clothes, and not rather a new wearer of clothes. . . . If you have any enterprises before you, try it in your old clothes. All men want, not something to do with, but something to do, or rather something to be. Perhaps we should never procure a new suit, however ragged or dirty the old, until we have so conducted, so enterprised or sailed in some way, that we feel like new men in the old, and that to retain it would be like keeping new wine in old bottles. Our moulting season, like that of the fowls, must be a crisis in our lives.* Walden, 1:36

He's right. And I recognized then that the Gulf War was my crisis, my moulting season. You can hardly turn a page of *Walden* without coming across a drop-dead, laser-guided aphorism or diamond-hard truth. And yet, the cumulative effect is that Henry was not so much preparing himself for life—which among men is a long, improvisational song and dance, with a storyline sometimes comic, sometimes tragic—as he was preparing himself for a long, lonely eternity.

Brooding there in the desert, kicking camel shits around while I smoked and paced around my truck, I considered the fact that the boys in the Pound cared for me *just because*—I was a Marine, they were Marines; I was a man, they were men. In looking down at my deliberately marked-up copy of *Walden*, underlined and highlighted and numbered and annotated—all clues to a map whose nature and use I still have not determined—I realized that I had loved a book more than any human. And I could no longer put my full faith in Thoreau's words in the chapter "Solitude,"

Nothing can rightly compel a simple and brave man to a vulgar sadness.
While I enjoy the friendship of the seasons I trust that nothing can make
life a burden to me.

Walden, 5:4

I distrusted him—but did not disbelieve that he meant what he said. I just sensed that he was either defective in some essential human longing or was whistling in the wind to avoid thinking of what he lost long ago. For the fact is, we are *politikon zoon*—political animals, as Aristotle said—and to simple and brave men, the death of a parent, or of a son, or a deep friend; or the divorce of one's parents; or abuse by a spouse or mother or father; or betrayal by a pal or a government—any of these, and far more, can rightly compel him to a vulgar sadness. They can bring him to his knees with grief and make him doubt his own senses.

Hatch, Farmer, Ebbers, Riley, and the Rat all brought greetings from the Pound that night. The brothers *was* hookin' me up. I loved those guys. When morning came, I walked out into the desert to take a piss. The entire desert floor, previously mottled with dried brown shrubs and grasses, had turned a wild green following the night's rain.

When I returned to my truck, one of the white captains from the Philadelphia reserve unit was weaving down the road in a semi, with Ebbers riding shotgun.

"Hey, Professa," called Ebbers, "I came to give you a break. You go on back to the Pound and get yourself a nice hot shower and some of that good ol' Marine Corps biscuits and gravy, hear?"

I rode back to Jubayl with the captain, who had always wanted to drive a "big rig." He said he figured now that the Iraqis were taken out, it was safe for him to be on the road practicing. I had been awake more or less continuously for almost twenty-four hours, but I still couldn't sleep because the captain couldn't shift for shit, and insisted on driving five hundred RPMs past redline all the way back to the port. So I looked out at the desert, now a profusion of vitality. As with the highway signs, and my marked-up copy of *Walden*, I lacked the means to do anything with this new life spread before me.

Prisoners of War

OUR GROUND WAR lasted one hundred hours. I had pulled all-nighters longer than that in college. But nothing I could have read in that span would strike me with sadness like our secret mission and its aftermath did. If the numbers of Iraqi POWs were right—and we'd heard around a hundred thousand—the Marines were processing surrendered Iraqi soldiers at a rate of a thousand an hour. They were just streaming through the desert, looking for someone to whom they could give themselves up. How can I communicate the sight of them? The alternations of grim hilarity, sadness, disgust, surprise, exhaustion, and horror that comprised the range of our emotions as we lived under the dark clouds of smoke from the oil fires burning just north of the camps, across the border in Kuwait? I can tell this story again and again, in all the ways I know how to tell a story, and still doubt that I've done it justice. But I *can* tell it again and again.

I had been standing in the middle of a ragged row of half-shaven Marines resting at ease. That day, I expected that I would drive another ten, sixteen, or twenty hours. The next day, too. The drooping brim of my boonie cover barely shielded my eyes from the morning sun, barely allowed me to see Gunny Benson roaming before our formation as he passed the word. We were shiftless because the end of the war hadn't changed anything for us. Our war carried the momentum of a trailer hauling 155 mm rounds, pushed forward in the deep ruts of a supply line still flowing northward from half-emptied ships at the port of Jubayl. We stood at attention beneath the Arabian sun, cupping lit cigarettes in our palms, shifting back and forth, adjusting our rifles on our shoulders. Then Gunny Benson spoke.

"Awright gentlemen, I need some volunteers for a secret mission."

"Volunteer?" asked Ebbers. "Ask Farmer."

Volunteer—the most derided word in the military, representing head cleaning, guard duty, and general servitude. So Bones asked, "This ain't no shit-suckin' mission, is it, Gunny?"

"I can't tell you what the mission is till you fuckin' volunteered for it, Bones. It's *secret.*"

"Shit, I ain't goin' then," replied Bones.

"Hey, Professor? You wanna go on a secret mission with me?" asked Hatch.

"Who—*me?*"

"We got any other Professors 'round here?"

Gunny Benson, interrupting us, announced, "Bones, Ebbers, Hatch, and Turnipseed: Y'all just volunteered."

At two o'clock, the four of us arrived at the company office. It was empty. A mini-bus was parked nearby. Painted lime green and lemon yellow, the bus was just this side of the shit-can: leaning hard on wear-whitened tires that bulged. A man so black he challenged the color spectrum leaned against the open bus door, skin shimmering like oil in sunlight. He wore faded jeans, a short-sleeved polyester work shirt, and a baseball cap, using both hands to hold up his cigarette.

Gunny Benson swung out from behind him, bald head poking out past the folded doors.

"Hey, gentlemen, grab your trash and get on up here for your briefing."

"Gunny, why we gonna have a briefing on a bus?"

"I'm waitin' for ya . . ." he said.

We climbed aboard the bus, packs jamming in the doorway. It was stifling—we gagged on the heat and the sickly smell of hot plastic seats, exhaust, and too many late-night cigarettes smoked on the road to Mecca.

"Gentlemen, this here's David. He's going to take your asses up north. You'll learn more about this here *secret mission* when you get there." With that, the gunny whirled around the front handrail and out into the midday breeze.

"Hey, brotha Dave, *you* know where we're going?" asked Bones.

David, pulling the door shut, said nothing and started the bus.

"Bones, this dude don't even speak English," said Ebbers. "How come we got to get the New York taxi driver all the way over here in the desert? Fuck this shit already."

Hatch and I quickly lowered those windows on which the tabs weren't stuck. As the bus jerked its way through the tent camp and out onto the Abu Hadriyah, we sat down, resigned to the long haul ahead.

We slept, awoke, smoked, made jokes, and stared at refinery stacks, the sand dunes with their filigree of scrub brush, and the occasional convoy passing back to the rear. Rain fell in small, dust-effacing streaks at first, then made a palimpsest of the finger-etched graffiti: the cartoon likenesses of Kilroy, Peace, and the brotherman-in-crosshairs logo of Public Enemy.

We stopped at zero-dark-thirty beside a small collection of warehouses. The weather had relaxed into a light drizzle. The desert air along the horizon was so dark with soot, dust, and clouds that the night seemed impenetrable. Set against this were our trucks—the likes of which we had seen, if ever, only in the pages of *National Geographic*. They bore some resemblance to old farm trucks—say, '62 Fords—with gaudily painted slats built up around the bed. Upon these slats were mounted: smashed soda cans, old Mercedes hubcaps, Arabic calligraphy . . . carnival trucks gone to seed.

A soaking wet staff sergeant waited for us. He held out a stick, from which dangled well-worn and water-stained crimson paper locker tags and the burnished bronze keys they identified.

"Now, the license number, and you're prob'ly gonna have to look pretty hard, is on the tag and on the key. I'm gonna hand 'em out, an' then I want you to make a quick walk-around of your trucks. After that, we're getting out of here."

We stood silently, packs on our backs, with David standing just inside the bus door, looking on, smoking. The staff sergeant added nothing about our destination or mission.

"Well, come get your keys, Marines."

Walking past him, shoulders slumped, we each pulled a key and its tag from the steel rod. As we passed, he would nod in affirmation. Of what? Our *mission?* We were too tired to ask.

I let my thoughts wander through all channels as I drove, sublime and absurd, chanting silently in my head:

> *Half-awake, half-awake,*
> *Half-awake we drove,*
> *On through the pouring rain,*
> *Drove the four of us.*

> *Forward the secret mission,*
> *Damned if we weren't dismayed.*
> *Not like we didn't know,*
> *In speaking we'd blundered.*
> *Ours not to figure why,*
> *Ours was a smart reply,*
> *Ours but to drive or die,*
> *On in our secret mission*
> *Drove the four of us.*

> *Desert to the left of us,*
> *Desert to the right of us,*
> *Desert in front of us,*
> *Rained on and thundered, etc., etc., etc., etcetera.*

And then the rain picked up again, beating hard against the windshield as the jaws of Death stifled a yawn, as tired of it all as we were. I leaned forward against the steering wheel, nose to the windshield, trying to make sense out of the blur. My truck rolled up and down the raised berms at road's edge. The truck ahead of me jerked to a stop. Slam. On the brakes. Jerk—jerk—jerk forward until I stopped against the bumper of the trailer ahead of me—took the cigarette, still burning, out of the folds of my trousers—slumped my shoulders, then waited in the silent darkness.

To my great surprise, the smoking of a single cigarette brought dawn to the horizon. A POW camp. The size of two football fields. Surrounded by hurricane fence topped with rolls of barbed wire. From each of the corners rose a wooden watchtower. It was right out of *Stalag 17* or *Hogan's Heroes*.

Two men stood together in the rain, staring through the fence at my truck. I could barely make out their faces, wrought with deep, mud-marked wrinkles. They were Iraqis, but wearing American-issue desert night parkas, dark green camouflaged with black stripes and splotches. Suddenly both men smiled, then chuckled, without even looking at each other, Vladimir and Estragon in an Iraqi POW camp—laughing at me in the rain, ankle deep in mud. Behind them, in the middle of the camp, stood a few dozen GP Mediums, their tent flaps raised to let in the rain and prevent any unseen monkey business. Along one fence, a couple of long, wooden pavilions sheltered the sick. All the tents were marked with the white and red insignias of the Red Cross and Red Crescent. Hundreds, possibly thousands, of men stood in the mud, yearning for a cigarette and something to eat, warm shelter and to get their boots, if they wore them, out of the mud. Maybe take a leak. I looked up from lighting another cigarette and Vladimir and Estragon had disappeared.

These weren't enemies! They were caricatures of enemies: they were *Haggard Shoulders Stooped* and *Heads Bowed*, laughing against rain and defeat . . . laughing. Inside one of the pavilions some Iraqis lay upon long tables, others slouched in a long line outside the mess tent.

As I sat in my truck, looking through and listening to the spatter-patter on the hood and windshield, I was mesmerized and let my cigarette burn to a butt.

"Hey, Professa, you just gonna sit there and daydream? Get them silly ashes off yourself."

"Ebbers?" Of course, *Ebbers*, one of the guys I drove up with; one of the *guys*, the unflappable comic rap-able *brothas*. "Oh shit, hey, Eb. No. What're we supposed to do now?"

"We got to meet some Red Cross liaison. He's s'posed to tell us what we do after he breaks down the Geneva Convention for us. We get to eat, too."

"MRES or hot?"

"MMMMM-HMM, M—R—E," he said, "*Meal, Ready-to-Eat.* Campbell's in camouflage; Popeye's in plastic."

I looked to my left, at the POWS, then to Ebbers. *A joke is the tombstone of feeling.*

A minute later I stepped into the rain and walked to a tent where I found Ebbers, Hatch, Bones, the staff sergeant, and a few other guys sitting at two picnic tables. Standing before them, hands clasped at parade rest, was another staff sergeant, this one fresh-faced and freckled.

". . . What that means, in plain English, is 'Don't feed the animals' and 'Don't put your hand in the cage.'" Not a bad recap of the Geneva Conventions. For my part, I had better sleep to do.

"Hey, Marine! You," he shouted, "you there. You with the glasses. Stand up! These are serious rules I'm explaining."

So I slept leaning against the tent post. As I struggled to stay vertical, my mind wandered back out to the camp.

Was this the shit?

Death is so much stranger when it's happening all around you, anonymously, randomly, in SCUD attacks and truck accidents and friendly fire incidents.

I wasn't sure if this *was* the shit, but it had the depth and resonance. If it was, it was different than I'd expected: it was some laughing abyss that I was supposed to stare down—and enemy as much within as without, and there was as much ambiguity in the emotions running through me as anything. I had no clear feelings of flight or fascination. And so it was with the whole war: I had dreams sometimes about taking a bullet in the shoulder, say, but nothing serious, no punctured lung or nerve damage. What's a bullet like that compared to all the other injuries that we suffer, and that can't be healed with a thread and needle? What if I lost my trust in the world forever? That would be an infinitely greater loss than, say, my hearing or a foot. Is there a color of heart you wear on your chest when your *head* gets fucked up? If there was, it would have to be dark grey—not quite black, and we'd just call it the Human Heart for Combat.

The air outside filled with the salt-cured stink of humans too long in the desert. Three cattle cars had arrived at the camp, loaded with Iraqis. The drivers of the semis that pulled the cars, long trailer beds with raised wooden rails, had left, leaving the POWs, still shut up in the cars, for our entertainment. *Do not take pictures of the enemy, this is considered degrading, and is prohibited.* First thing out the door? A photo session. Ebbers and Hatch and the rest of the convoy lined up, joined by Marines from who-the-fuck-knows-where, posing: arms thrown around each other's shoulders and thumbs raised, one man peeling off the end of the group and another joining in at the other end, like a photo session turned Chinese fire drill. *Do not offer the prisoners food or drink (or cigarettes).* "Hey, man, you see how high that guy jumped to get that Coke?" After the photo op, the guys took turns tossing Cokes and cigarettes and MREs into the groping and outstretched arms of the Iraqis. *Treat the enemy as a human being, due all the accord and respect that you as a fellow human being would ask for yourself.* After the Cokes, cigarettes, and dehydrated MRE fruit packets were gone, everyone milled around the trucks, walking up close, right up to the rails of the cattle cars: "Hey, you speak English?" "How come you didn't just kill ol' Saddam?" To one man, who for some reason was clutching his groin, someone yelled out, "Hey dude, ain't you already scared enough you pissed your pants? Or are you just workin' it?"

I couldn't find the words to protest. But neither could I grab-ass, joke, fuck around, and enjoy the carnival. I looked up at the prisoners' ashen, hollow eyes, their limbs, shrunken from long and desperate months of bare sustenance. All of them seemed to be struggling to stand, and to smile, but ashamed despite their smiles. Indeed, only the successful beggars grinned. Those over whose heads the occasional new cigarette would pass shrank visibly at the lost opportunity.

My vanquished were now vanquishing me. I wanted to get a picture, too, if only to remember the image later, to fix it on paper, *objectively;* so that I could understand at one remove, or not at all, to look at myself standing before a forty-foot tractor-trailer bed filled with hollow men.

But I did not stay for a photo. I walked back to my truck. My vague dread returned, taking up a solid stand just below or behind my diaphragm, so that I couldn't comfortably release a full breath. My eyes and body ached for sleep, but when I climbed up into my cab I reflexively took up my portable Nietzsche, flipping pages to find "The Gay Science." I strained to pay attention for the reward of an aphorism:

> 48. Knowledge of misery.—*Perhaps there is nothing that separates men or ages more profoundly than a difference in their knowledge of misery: misery of the soul as well as the body. Regarding the latter we moderns may well be, all of us, in spite of our frailties and infirmities, tyros who rely on fantasies, for lack of any ample firsthand experience . . . regarding the misery of soul, I now look at every person to see whether he knows this from experience or only from descriptions; whether he still considers it necessary to simulate this knowledge, say, as a sign of refinement, or whether at the bottom of his soul he no longer believes in great pains of the soul and has much the same experience when they are mentioned that he has at the mention of great physical sufferings, which make him think of his own toothaches and stomach-aches.*

I put the book in my lap and watched the windshield, dried with streaks of dust where rain dribbled from the roof. Our twentieth century was not Nietzsche's nineteenth. If only he had seen the Somme,

Auschwitz, Hiroshima, the gulags, or the Killing Fields . . . Romanticism, and its peculiar agonies, seemed as dead as Nietzsche's "God."

And yet, for all that, I imagined the horror of war while still watching it, one of his dilettantes. My imagination ran jump-cuts of those who were not here: those charred in their tanks, crushed beneath a bunker, or devastated by a five-thousand-pound bomb.

Perhaps we should say, "Der Tod ist tot." *Death is dead.* It seems like such an unlikely thing to wish for, now—or ever. The wind picked up, whistling through my truck.

"Thu*nnkk!*" A metallic knock resounded within my cab.

"Hey, Professor, get your butt out your truck," called Hatch.

The POWs were walking past us now, a grim procession of soot, grime, dried blood, matted and greasy hair, dead and distant stares, hollow cheeks, the meek and wretched going to the collection of their inheritance. Now that I could see them face to face, these were men in their thirties, some in their forties. Our eyes did not meet. I was so tired that I grew dizzy from the strain of avoiding them. Some were wounded, some not. I looked at their jaws, slack to a man, at their scars, ubiquitous and pink—or grey with age, from the Iran-Iraq war. I followed a scar from the base of an ear to the cracked skin at the corner of an eye, an eye barely turning in my direction, an eye shunning my gaze. Who had honor? Probably none of us. Though visibly haggard ourselves, we looked guiltily healthy. They walked defeat. Sometimes, approaching the wide-open gates of the camp, an Iraqi would begin to trot, arms jangling, chin jauntily raised, but trot without the energy to break into a jog, or an easy shuffle—it was either a stumble or a tortured, comical trot. Like the POW camp was Disneyland and they had passed the height requirement for the ride.

Secret mission! Standing before them in the clearing haze, I half-wished that I was working the pump truck, sucking shit from Satellites on Camp Shepard. But only half-wished, fascinated.

The grim staff sergeant, waddling on soaked bowlegs, approached our huddle, bringing the show to a stop. "Okay, gentlemen, I've just received word that you're going to be relieved," he said.

"We just got here," said Ebbers.

"Yeah, what's up with that?" asked Hatch.

"I don't know. Maybe they need you down at Jubayl. Corporal over there will drive you down as soon as you get your gear loaded onto the bus. Leave the keys in the trucks you drove up here."

Our secret mission ended as a day-and-a-half long exercise in exasperation and dismay, despair and exhaustion. As we drove, the sun burned the skies, making room for the wind to replace the rain with black smoke and soot from the oil fires. By the time we reached Camp Shepard late in the afternoon, having been up for more than thirty hours, and on the road for more than twelve, I could barely stand in line for a hot meal.

Smoking a cigarette by the Gulf, away from the guys in the Pound, away from the POWs, I felt as if I'd come up short. I felt disgust at my ignorance, at my inability to put a word or thought to my experience. I lit another cigarette and, while watching the smoke disappear into the breeze, I understood what was the right word, what the right thought, the proper opinion and perfect gesture: Nothing.

The next day I learned that one of the guys from Minneapolis, Corporal Joseph, was killed when his tractor flipped on one of the highways up north. I got the day off to hitch a ride and attend the memorial service, up in Mishab.

Instead I spent the day smoking and reading by the remnants of our bunker up at Saudi Motors. No one had done a thing with it since we had watched it crash down around us. The rain and wind had worked the loose sand into the cracks and seams along the tarmac, making it look like an ancient ruin of itself.

In the afternoon, I went to the Conex railcar that served as a little movie house: a large-screen TV and a VCR with a bunch of wooden benches lined up in front of it. You could rent videos at the tent next door. I rented *Empire of the Sun* and watched it alone.

That night, we learned about the "Highway of Death," the six-lane highway from Kuwait City to Basra on which those Iraqis who hadn't been killed or turned themselves in as POWs were frantically trying to escape. U.S. fighter planes and helicopter gunships blew up the highway on either side of the streaming traffic of Iraqi deserters, then killed everything that moved in between. They left miles of burnt-out tanks, trucks, buses and bodies.

This was a brand new flavor of fucked-up, served cold. Having seen the Iraqi POWs in their cattle cars; having avoided their eyes, it was hard for us to consider them our enemies. It was hard, thinking of their slaughtered brothers, not to remember other injustices—whether they occurred at Fort Pillow or Tuskeegee or My Lai. We never saw hate in their eyes. More like regret and relief. The whole rain-washed affair had been subdued, tired, carried out in the haze of exhaustion, most definitely, but not in the grip of malice.

"That's some-motherfucking-thing else," said Ebbers. "Brothers running away and we go and shoot them in the back. A big green fifty-caliber weenie coming down out the sky to fuck you to death. Ain't no fuckin' way."

"Yo, Ebbers—when they was shootin' SCUDs at you, you weren't talking like that," said Luke.

"You hear any alarms, Luke?" shouted Ebbers. "Shit, just like a white man to say something like that."

The tent fluttered with *sotto voce* echoes of "Damn, brother." It was my turn.

"Say, Professor," called Hatch, "What you think of that fucked up shit?"

"I think," I said, "that the idea of 'enemy' is much more easily borne in the abstract—through the distant chain of hierarchy and command. That enemies, on the other hand, have more than one means of defeat— especially when disarmed. In the long run, our actions on that highway will come back to haunt us."

"Yeah?" asked Bones. "You still ain't said what you think—you even worse than Luke, Turnipstrudel. Some kind of poli-fuckin'-tician."

"Well, Bones," I replied, "maybe I should have just acknowledged Hatch—I think that shit is fucked up. What more do you want me to say?"

We spent the next two weeks in silence, driving alone through the desert.

Reunion

ᴇᴀʀʟʏ ɪɴ ᴛʜᴇ ᴍᴏʀɴɪɴɢ of March 18, we were awakened by the holler-ing of Gunny Benson.

"Awright gentlemen, get up, get up! We got to get movin' this mornin."

Behind the gunny's sun-framed shadow, the waiting five-tons rumbled at idle.

"Shit, Gunny, what time is it?" asked Ebbers.

"'S'time to get your ass out of here and load your trash on the trucks, that's what fuckin' time it is," yelled the gunny as he disappeared through the tent flaps.

We could hear his muffled roar through the canvas, calling other men from their tents. In the faint blue light, men began to roll out of their racks, silently gathering their gear into bundles. I rolled over and went back to sleep.

"Hey, Professor, pack your shit—we got to be on the move."

It was Mountain Man, who stood against the now barren canvas of our tent. Everyone but me had packed up their things and loaded them on the truck. I sat up, reaching for a cigarette.

"Just a minute, Mountain Man, I gotta have breakfast here."

Hatch came in, and Ebbers followed.

"Here we go, Professor," said Hatch, "why don't you go and smoke that nasty thing outside while we gather up your trash."

The tent was strewn with litter: black plastic bags, a row of liter bottles filled with piss, broken pack straps, shoelaces, cardboard boxes from ᴍʀᴇꜱ. As I stepped outside, I noticed the absence of piss and mildew smells. I hadn't even finished my cigarette when Hatch and Ebbers and

Mountain Man walked out with my gear: three seabags, an ALICE pack, and a cot, disassembled and neatly folded.

"Professa, why don't you put on the rest of your stuff and get up here," called Ebbers, now sitting on the troop seat of a fully loaded five-ton.

I stepped back into the tent one last time. My flak jacket with the H-harness lay in a vestigial sprawl; my helmet, gas mask, and my rifle lay nearby amidst the garbage. I picked them up and breathed deeply: moving out and moving on. Again—same old motherfuckin' shit.

After a short drive past the refineries skirting Jubayl, we arrived at our new home: an endless array of abandoned tents pitched on sand-covered concrete platforms. The surveyed rows of platforms stretched a half-mile into the desert. Lining the main road through the camp were two rows of shacks: shitters and showers. The showers were made of fifty-five-gallon drums torched in two and punctured with holes, mounted on stud frames. Plywood sheets sheathed the frames from knee height to shoulders to cover the privates, with one sheet held fast by hinges and a hook: the door. The toilets merely reversed the arrangement: a half drum sat beneath a plywood sheet with a hole cut in it, and a stud frame held plywood rising up to the belly-button. The exception being that the open areas of the shitter frame were covered with window screen. Even so, a tall man would have to sit down to avoid pissing into the wind. I took an archeological attitude toward the camp, especially toward the curiously contructed "Marine Corps Muscle Beach," as the crudely painted sign called it. In the midst of one row of tents, a platform had been left vacant, and standing on this platform were weight benches made of two-by-fours, as well as squat racks, pull-up bars, and a leg-lift—all made of two-by-fours and pallet scraps. The barbells were simply two-by-fours with deep grooves hacked into the ends, onto which sandbags filled to varying degrees with sand could be hung.

We were the first to arrive at this ghost camp, and spent the morning and afternoon sweeping sand from the cool floors of the tents and out onto the walkways, where bare comm lines and electrical wiring snaked from tent to tent. We took pallets left haphazardly around the camp and used them as doorstops, and hung cardboard signs marking the billeting over the flaps of the incoming units' future homes. The guys from the Dog Pound made a sign for themselves, listing the membership of the reunited Pound, some of whose original members would be returning from up north. While they were making their sign, I had the job of marking the three tents designated for the Minneapolis men, in one of which I had already claimed a coveted corner. When we were finished, we gathered again at the Pound for a dinner of MRES and bottled water.

"Hey, Professa," said Flowers, "Check this out—"

He held up the large sign he was drawing for the Dog Pound, on which he had written in crude gothic letters the names and rank of the members. At the bottom, in large script, it said:

HONORARY MEMBER: L/CPL TURNIPSEED—"THE PROFESSOR"

This concrete listing marked the end of my membership in the Pound, and even during the dinnertime joking, I could feel the door closing.

We were interrupted by a familiar, forgotten voice:

"Hey, Turnip, where's our tents?"

"Solter! How've you been?" I leaped up from the floor, and stared with the rest of the Pound at the dusty person before us: still draped in tent-flap, Solter was not so much covered as suffused with dust and sand. He looked as if he hadn't showered in a month. He probably hadn't.

"I'm okay," he said. "You the only one here?"

"No, I'm just sitting in here with a bunch of invisible men—what the fuck, Solter, can't you see *black?*"

Even Bones let out a peal of bass laughter.

"I meant," he replied, flustered, "I meant are you the only one from Minneapolis, dummy."

"Is someone else supposed to be here?" I asked.

"Uh-huh," replied Solter, "a whole busload of guys. They left Mishab an hour before we did, and we're the rear party."

"Well, boys," I said to the Pound, "I guess I gotta show Solter here to his tent."

"Keep in touch, Professor," said Hatch.

"Don't go an' disappear on us," said Ebbers.

"Okay, my brothas," I said. Standing next to Solter, it didn't feel right: they were starting to fade for me, too.

As Solter and I walked back along the row to the Minneapolis tents, several battered buses, followed by a rumbling cloud of five-ton trucks, turned off the highway, whining to a stop fifty yards ahead of us.

"They're here!" shouted Solter.

He broke into a quick stride, and I followed him. Men jumped, stepped, streamed, hopped, dropped, and climbed out of the buses and trucks like bugs evading an exterminator. Then they climbed back in and on to get their gear, as if the film of the extermination was being played backwards, except for the smokers, who were huddled in groups. Out of this swarm I began to pick out faces: Bergman, Solter, Sergeant Bernie and Schlitz; Sergeant Burt, our only woman Marine, whom I hadn't talked to once during the entire war, and who was already carrying her bags to the isolation of the WM tent; Clem and Heinemann; Landers and Boomer chatting with Gunny Benson; these and a dozen other men stooped beneath their cots and rifles and seabags.

I caught up with Clem and Heinemann on their way back from the WM tents, envying the well-worn desert night parkas draped casually over their shoulders.

"Hey, guys!" I called, "How was your camping trip?"

"Turnipseed?! Where'd you come from? We figured you went UA, you know, drove your truck to Paris or something," said Clem.

"No, but now that you mention it—"

"Where's our tents, Turnip?" asked Heinemann.

"Right over there," I said, pointing, "Hey?! How'd *you* get up North, Heinemann?"

"I left, like, a week after you got off guard. What? Didn't you miss me?"

"Guess not. You know, trying to keep track of everyone over here is like trying to follow the characters in a Russian novel."

"Turnipseed—haven't changed a bit, huh?" said Clem, "It's good to see you."

"You too," I said, "you too."

"Burt's got a night parka for you," Clem added. "Why don't you go catch up with her."

"You guys really got one for me?" I asked. It was stupid, but I really, really wanted one of those damned parkas. When I saw all the Iraqis wearing them up at Kibrit, I thought I'd never get one.

"Yeah, we lost a pallet of 'em on a Red Cross supply run. You know, an accident. You didn't think we'd let the Iraqis have 'em before we'd give you one, did you, Turnip?"

I felt too guilty to say that I had, and ran after Sergeant Burt like a silly puppy.

When the lights went out for the night, I lay in my cot, taking in the strangeness of my old familiarity: the old dislikes, hostilities, and lack of understanding. I thought of all the friends I'd lost throughout my life— so many uprootings, so many changes of heart and mind. I looked out over my chest, through the tent flaps at the light shining through the seams of the dispatch office tent. The shadows cut undulating furrows of light into the boot-pocked sand. In the air, the muffled cacophony of reunions sounded through the night.

Next door, a few Minneapolis guys were huddled around a cot, playing a fierce round of poker.

"So, are you in or what?"

"I suppose. I mean, yeah, I'm in."

"Check your *cojones,* Solter, 'cause I got four tens."

"Does that beat a straight?"

Laughs rose like devils for the doomed.

"Well, I mean, one of those straights where they're all the same kind, like diamonds?"

"Fuck, Solter. You are one lucky motherfucker. A straight-fucking-flush?"

"Does that mean I win?"

The Dog Pound was housed nearby; their voices drifted over, too.

"Luke, Luke, get your stinky-ass, toxic gas feet into your sleepin' bag. I mean, I thought ya loved me, Luke? Why you trying to kill me like this?"

"Fuck off, Mountain Man," cried Luke. "You got used to it in the other tent."

"Hey, Luke, take it easy," called Ebbers, "we your Pound brothers—we love your stinky ass. C'mon: When I say Dog you say Poun'!— Dog . . ."

"Poun'!"

"Dog, Dog!"

"Poun,' Poun'!"

"Awright, lemme hear y'awl!"

"Ooh, ooh, ooh, ooh!"

Ebbers broke into a rap and Sergeant Bernie rose from his cot, yelling to no one in particular, "I sure as hell wish they'd shut up!"

He looked toward me, glaring in accusation.

"What, I'm no accomplice," I said.

"Yeah, well," he grumbled, "I just wish that you'd go tell 'em to shut the hell up."

"What? Does that mean you're going to go tell Heinemann and Solter and Blegen to shut up? I mean, what the fuck is that?"

"Well, our guys are playing cards. They're just yapping for nothing."

I looked him square in the eye. "Bullshit."

He nodded, as if to say, "You're right—my bad. But I'm too tired to go there . . ."

He dropped himself back onto his cot, then turned angrily into his pillow. I tried the same, but I had come down with a sinus and respiratory infection. Whenever I lay on my side, my lungs and sinuses would drain like an egg timer of contentment: two minutes, then roll over and ease the other side. Two minutes, roll over. Two minutes, roll over. Two minutes, roll over.

I rose from my cot and walked out into the night. I carried with me my book bag, and sported with pride my new desert night parka—with liner. After a short walk out to the fifty-five-gallon-drum shitters, I peeked into the empty company office tent: two desks, two chairs, a light bulb with chain, a Bunsen burner, and a new box of MREs. Promising.

They had managed to procure a water cooler at the dispatch tent next door, so I walked over to fill my canteen for coffee water. One of the Dallas captains reclined in his chair, with a stack of Q-Tips and pipe cleaners strewn across his desk. He clenched a cigar in his teeth while he held his Beretta to his eye, pointing it toward the bare bulb hanging from the beam. A red-haired WM sergeant from Dallas spit tobacco as she updated the status board. Neither of them looked up at me as I stepped to the cooler.

After digging around in an already savaged care package for something interesting to snack on, I looked over at the captain, now assiduously scrubbing his 9 mm.

"Excuse me, sir—you haven't seen a *New Republic* lying around, have you?"

"Who wants to know?" he asked, eyes fixed on his weapon.

"I do. It was mine, the one with Norman Schwarzkopf on the cover?"

He looked up. "Turnipseed? I figured that was your communiss trash. I shit-canned it."

"You shit-ca—? never mind," I said, trying not to look desperate as I glanced at the wastebasket filled with Q-Tips and pipe cleaners.

"It ain't in there, Turnipseed. I tole you, I *shit-canned* it, where it belongs."

"Belongs! It belongs to me."

"Not anymore. We don't tolerate faggot crap like that around here."

"Are you fu—."

"I'm finished," he said. "Now why don't you go back next door. You are on duty, aren't you?"

I lurched, then caught myself. "Duty?" I wasn't officially on duty, but it quickly occurred to me that this was a one-time special offer from the Fates: there was no night duty, but I was about to create the post and the appointment, with the captain's implicit permission.

"Yes, *duty*. You *are* night duty, aren't you?"

"Yeah. Of course."

Seren-fuckin'-dipity, but I wish he hadn't thrown away my *New Republic*. I was interrupted from my Taster's Choice and *Seven Pillars of Wisdom* only once during the night, when the captain came to check on me. I spent the rest of the time writing letters, reading, jotting notes in my journals, and, occasionally, stepping outside for a cigarette beneath the clear Arabian sky.

After almost sixty days of war, we had three dead, a dozen or so injured, and of more than a thousand trucks leased from Saudi civilians, we turned in just a few hundred. Now we tarried, playing volleyball, playing poker or playing sick. I wasn't playing—I was sick, hacking up lung cookies and wheezing in chunks. The only way I could keep from coughing was to chain smoke. I had a fever. I couldn't eat, even though we had finally gotten a chow hall, with hot catered food, set up out past the volleyball nets.

I slept through the hot days. I usually rose from my stupor near evening chow, when everyone came stomping and crashing through the tent after work. We were still trying to find the couple dozen trucks we were sure we hadn't trashed, and to fix as many as we could to save a few dimes for Uncle Sucker. Even though we didn't give a damn about saving money for the Corps and its Uncle, we had been deprived so long from real mechanics' labor that we really went at it. Even me, before I got sick. After work, a half-dozen of us would gather around Heinemann's cot to play poker: five-card draw, seven-card stud, Texas Hold 'Em, Arizona, Guts, and the occasional hand of blackjack if the dealer was running low on funds.

We used an upturned plywood cable-wheel as our table, and cash for bets. Heinemann sat on his cot, Blegen usually to his right. Solter to the right of Blegen, a guest from Memphis or Philly or Dallas next to Solter (sometimes an extra in Solter's place if he had heard from his wife that day), then me, then another guest between me and Heinemann's left. Since the game and the dealer rotated around the table, where you sat didn't matter much, strategically. Still, it was good to sit across from Heinemann, because he was the true connoisseur of poker, like one of Gibbon's barbarians: intelligent and cunning, but with animal instincts intact. Fear, aggression, hope, failure, confidence—his own heart's, and the others'—registered themselves in finely perceptible gestures of brow and eye, like a dog who clearly knows that he is his master's master. You liked to keep an eye on him, his trademark smirks—you didn't know whether he was bluffing or had a hand, but at least you *knew* when you were fucked.

We were waiting for Solter to get back from calling his wife, so we BS'ed.

"You guys play like this up North?" I asked.

"Oh, yeah," crowed Heinemann, "I already sent home two grand. Too bad we couldn't have been in camp together more often—I'd probably already have four."

"Hey, Heinemann and Blegen! You, too, Turnip. Listen to this. My mom says the Minnesota legislature is considering a bill to give the Gulf War vets two free years of college. What do you think of that, Turnip, two free years of philosophy?"

"That would be great," I said, "but I'll wait until it's passed to celebrate."

"I don't know," said Clem, "my mom says everyone she's talked to supports it. I guess we're really big heroes back home."

"Two years of college? She say anything about private schools?" asked Heinemann, who went to Macalester.

"I mean, c'mon guys," I protested, aching with hope, "let's wait until we get home and they find out that our heroism consisted of crashing trucks and getting lost."

Clem looked up. "You got lost, too, Turnip?"

"Yeah, I spent like a day and a half driving around Saudi Arabia: out into the middle of the desert, back up along the Gulf. I got stuck, I got lost, I don't think I slept for like, two days."

"You hear about the time we got lost?"

"Oh, man, this is a good one!" howled Heinemann.

"Yeah, Turnip," said Clem, "It was pretty fucked up. We were on this run, me and Boomer and Heinemann, and Solter, I think, and we took a wrong turn somewhere. We had to camp for the night by the side of the road. We didn't know where the hell we were."

Heinemann leaned forward from the edge of his cot. "I mean, no-fucking-where, Turnipseed. We were so far out in the desert a camel couldn't have gotten to us."

"So Boomer has us on firewatch all night, locked and loaded," resumed Clem, "and the next morning, right after the sun comes up on the horizon, these Cobras come cruising toward us like bats out of hell. I mean, it's like *Apocalypse Now* or something, right?"

"You surfed?"

"No, but this colonel jumps out, and he's just *screaming*, 'God-dammit, who's in charge of this clusterfuck.' Well, Boomer's only got the last piss drip of patience left, and he's not wearing a blouse, so he gets in this colonel's face, 'I'm the fuck in charge. What's *your* fuckin' problem?'"

Heinemann and Clem and Blegen thought this was the funniest thing in the world, bent over in laughter as Solter walked through the front of the tent.

"Oh, you guys tellin' that story about gettin' lost again?" he asked, "I love the look on people's faces when you tell 'em we were only a mile or something away from the Iraqis. D'you tell that part yet?"

Heinemann, Clem, and Blegen thought this was the stupidest of narrative interruptions, and glared at Solter, who made way for two more at the tent flaps: an Army sergeant and a spec-4 coated in so much dust they looked fryer-ready when they stepped into the tent. They held bulging seabags and wore the constipated expressions of door-to-door salesmen.

"You guys here for cards?" asked Heinemann "We could use some doggy money."

The sergeant, short but built like a nosetackle, cleared his throat for the pitch. "Actually, Marines, we're here to let you in on a unique opportunity. One time only. We have in these duffel bags some genuine Iraqi merchandise. If you are interested in acquiring these one-of-a-kind keepsake items, we will be showing them in the next tent."

"Follow me, Marines," said the sergeant, waving his buddy with the bags ahead of him.

Blegen called after them, "Hey, you guys see any shit?"

The sergeant half-turned, seductively. "Naw, by the time we got through, it was just a damned wasteland. A bunch of POWs wandering around. We got most of our merchandise while we were policing the dead bodies."

"You took this stuff from dead guys?" asked Solter.

"We'll be showing the merchandise in the next tent," said the sergeant. "That's all you need to know."

We debated for a while, then decided to postpone the card game. When Blegen and Heinemann and Solter and I got to the next tent, home to the Dallas Marines, we watched Blegen's protégé Junior hold a night-vision scope to his eye.

"Hey, Tex," said the sergeant, "I wouldn't open that lens cap in here—"

"Shee-it, that was bright," cried Junior, recoiling. "Can I take it outside for a minute?"

"Sure, go right on ahead," said the spec-4, "but you break it, you buy it."

"Hell, I'm gonna buy this som-bitch anyway. Perez, give the man two hundred dollars, I'm goin' out to play."

Two cots had been pushed together as a display table. There was another night-vision scope, a half-dozen pistols, piles of bayonets and knives, complete and incomplete sets of the propaganda booklets dropped by the Allies, insignia from various ranks and units, berets, helmets, epaulets, cartridge belts, canteens: it looked like an Iraqi uniform inspection crossed with a survivalists' fair. I half-expected these guys to start pulling out the really crazy shit, like ears and fingers.

I felt a little dizzy with shopper's frenzy—I especially wanted the Iraqi banknotes with propaganda cartoons on the back. Then a flash caught my eye, from the far corner of the tent. A man was bent over a scimitar, of all things, sharpening the blade. He was really going at it. He looked up at the Iraqi gear being sold by the soldiers, then turned to the guy at the next cot. "Damn if I couldn't get me a raghead."

I couldn't believe it. "Salerno!" I said. "What ever happened to all that happy horseshit about Jesus?"

Startled, he looked up, scimitar still in hand. He stared for a long second. When he recognized me, his face changed. He didn't say anything, and went back to his task.

"Salerno," one of the Dallas guys called out, "You a Jesus freak, too?"

"Yeah, he all kind of freak," said one of the others.

Salerno's head bobbed with every stroke of his sharpening steel. He wouldn't be talking anymore. I knew it and he knew it, but no one else in the tent did. I looked at him with tremendous sadness. I was not sad because he was, in his failed crusade, a victim of public humiliation and razzing. Shit, we all faced that regularly—we were Marines, after all. No, I was sad because, in the last glance of his eyes before they disappeared beneath the brim of his cover, I caught a look of recognition—of life's sad bargains, the moments when style crashes against reality; sad that he could not share the fucked-up pain of his daydreams and that I could not tell him that this was the truest life. In a tent packed with soldiers and Marines trading in the stuff of the dead, it seemed a pity that a moment so pure with life should pass so quietly, unnoticed.

The Army hucksters had to beat a quick retreat, because Staff Sergeant Landers walked in through the back of the tent unannounced, holding a clipboard.

"Okay, Marines, I got some word to pass here."

"We gotta take some more of those fucked-up pills?"

"No," he said, "no pills. We're going to start collecting your ammunition this evening, at the dispatch tent. There will be a log with your name on it, and two WM's will be counting your rounds. If you have lost any rounds, I want you to tell me now, so you don't waste any time in the dispatch tent. Anyone lose their rounds?"

"Shit, dude, I ain't even seen my rounds in, like, a month. Hey, Rivera, you seen my rounds?"

Solter had forgotten what a round was. "Rounds?"

"Bullets," said Bergman, "as in, 'Where the fuck are mine?'"

We had grown so accustomed to the daily grind of tractor-trailer driving, and so used to dragging our M-16's around, that it seemed strange to find that we had also been carrying NATO rounds—or not carrying them, and wondering where we'd stashed them for safekeeping.

Which isn't to say that we felt safe. Not driving tractor-trailers, which even in the United States is one of the most dangerous professions. We got word that yet another guy from our battalion, but not from our company, had died. I don't know what happened, exactly, the guy had been offloading a tank or bulldozer or something, and the ramp that swung down from the bed of the trailer struck him in the forehead, scooping his face and brains out like ice cream. Instant death.

When I awoke, late in the morning the day of the memorial service, the tent was already steaming. I was sick as a dog and couldn't breathe, so I had to taste the rancid socks and mildewed sleeping bags with each breath. It had only been about four hours since I'd tiptoed in from "night duty" in the company office. I was awakened by the obnoxious nasal haranguing of Staff Sergeant Landers.

"Hey, Turnipseed, Bernie said yer really sick. You need to go see a corpsman. You need a replacement for night duty?"

"I'll see a corpsman today. I can handle night duty."

"Yeah? Maybe we oughta call you the light-duty night duty."

It was such a great scam. I leaned over the edge of my cot, rubbing my eyes and scratching my head. There were little flowers of snot-crusted toiletpaper all over the sand beneath my cot. I looked down at Landers' dusty boots, one broken lace knotted halfway down the tongue. Landers meant well.

"Here's a chit for medical. Oh, and you better hurry if you're gonna make the service."

After Staff Sergeant Landers left, I was alone in the tent, listening to my heart pound and trying to ignore the pack of Camels poking into my ribs, the bar-end of my rack digging into my ankles. I knew it wasn't making me better, but for some reason a few drags on a smoke really toned down the death hack. I gave in and headed out for a smoke. The light outside the tent flaps was bright, white and flat against the dusty canvas.

I went to the medical tent on the way to the service. The corpsmen didn't have my medical records, so they gave me a piece of paper saying I had bronchitis and a fever of a hundred and one and had been given antibiotics and light duty. Since we didn't have any trucks left, pretty much everyone was on light duty: half our company was playing volleyball when I walked past them to the empty lot where they were holding the service.

As I sat on the bumper of a truck, I watched the chaplain prepare: shuffling papers, checking the microphone, fiddling around with the cassette player and only occasionally looking out at the few Marines beginning to gather. The sun flashed off the gold cross on his collar.

I was nervous. My stomach was tight from too much coffee and too many cigarettes—no food. I hadn't eaten in more than a day. My mouth was sour with bile and tobacco, pasty from dehydration. When had I last brushed my teeth? Several days? I reached for a canteen and shrugged as I rattled the few drops inside. This was the first memorial service I'd ever attended. The dozen or so Marines who turned out stepped into formation. I almost left. Then I stubbed out my cigarette, grinding against the gritty bumper of the five-ton against which I was leaning.

I tried, as I listened to the chaplain deliver his monotone service, to imagine that this was Corporal Joseph's service . . . to see the empty space in the formation where I should have been. Staring blankly at the chaplain, listening to the dull, scratchy recording of "Eternal Father," I imagined Joseph in his truck. Next to him his A-driver might have been laughing just before the truck flipped, cab bouncing forward, wedging him safely against the seat, but tossing Joseph out into the sand to be crushed beneath the full weight of the semi . . . *His* memorial. This is what it must have been like. The sun beaming down mercilessly, a couple dozen knees locked then unlocked, heels aching, throbbing inside baking boots, every twitch of nerve or slight shift in stance an evasion. The flags of the United States and of the Marine Corps would be flaccid in an almost imperceptible breeze. Behind and beside the formation would sit several dozen parked trucks, their bent and broken Mercedes badges a reminder to onlooking eyes of exhaustion and death.

The man was awarded a Navy Commendation Medal for his sacrifice. We only had a week left until we flew home.

Soldier's Tales

WE HAD TURNED IN OUR AMMUNITION; turned in our trucks. I was alone in the company office tent, bent over the desk reading. Next to me the Bunsen burner whispered small flames, and the tin canteen cup above them, just filled with water, rested cold and mute. Next door, in the dispatch office, I could hear someone at the status board, squeaking out the final tallies of trucks lost or destroyed. I leaned back in my chair, raising one knee against the edge of the desk, tilting *Seven Pillars of Wisdom* just enough to catch the light of the single dangling bulb:

> *We rode past the other bodies of men and women and four more dead babies, looking very soiled in the daylight, towards the village; whose loneliness we now knew meant death and horror. By the outskirts were low mud walls, sheepfolds, and on one something red and white. I looked close and saw the body of a woman folded across it, bottom upwards, nailed there by a saw bayonet whose haft stuck hideously into the air from between her naked legs. She had been pregnant, and about her lay others, perhaps twenty in all, variously killed, but set out in accord with an obscene taste.*

Our war was over, and excepting a few thousand POWs whose presence oppressed me beyond words, I had escaped without harm. I had witnessed no atrocities, and the deaths of the men in our battalion, including that of Corporal Joseph from Minneapolis, happened out of my sight. None of them had even come at the hands of the enemy. Rather than feeling lucky, I felt cheated—as if my war had been undermined or stolen from me.

I looked up from the book: Hatch and Phalen, a Philly guy who'd been detached to another unit earlier in the war, were standing in the doorway, watching me. Their shoulders drooped, and they did not so much walk into the tent, as pour themselves the few steps to my desk.

"Turnipseed?" Phalen asked. "You the duty around here?"

In my confusion, still trying to come to grips with Lawrence's ghastly scene, I had forgotten that I was merely skating, malingering with my books: "Yeah, I guess I'm duty."

"You guess, Professor?" asked Hatch, "Well, I sure as shit hope you're guessin' right, 'cause we got some problems. *Serious* shit."

Phalen shrugged. "This place," he said, dropping his tired Irish ass onto the desk. He didn't seem to think it was such serious shit. "We got pulled over by the MPs outside Camp Three."

"Check it out," said Hatch, "they said some dudes got waxed by rag-heads in a white Toyota. Terrorist incident—no shit."

"No, it's fucking shit," said Phalen, "and now they won't let us out on the road without our ammunition." When he stopped, his voice paused without finality, as if he were going to say something, but that he required the cigarette for which he was reaching in order to say it.

I finished his sentence as he paused for a light. "And we already turned in our ammunition, right?"

Hatch walked past me out the back of the tent, to wake Gunnery Sergeant Benson, who was our Staff NCO in charge for the evening. It was four A.M.

"What're you readin'?" asked Phalen, turning the book around on the desk. "Lawrence of Arabia? No shit. He wrote a book, too?"

"And translated Homer and dug up Carcamesh," I said, "among other things."

"Yeah? What's he say about this place?"

"He says it is beautiful and betrayed."

Behind us, Hatch and Gunny Benson entered. The gunny groaned like a man in his own house as he dropped himself into a chair behind the only other desk in the tent.

"Turnipseed?" he asked, "they really got you on night duty? Or are you just fuckin' around in here?"

"Actually, Gunny—"

"Actually, don't answer. I don't even wanna know."

"Has Corporal Hatch filled you in?"

"Oh, *suuure*, Corporal Hatch woke me up just so he could fill me right up to the ass with all the good news. What about *you?*"

"Actually, I was getting more information from Phalen before getting up to go tell—"

"The captain. *After* you finish your coffee and your cigarette, right?" asked the gunny, smiling. "Fuck it, I think I'll mess around with y'all. I never give a fuck 'bout anything at four in the mornin,' anyhow. You sharin' cigarettes tonight, Turnipseed?"

The gunny leaned back in his chair, and exhaled a grey plume. His little pot belly pressed gently against his grey sweatpants, his grey chest hairs puffed out beneath his faded maroon T-shirt, on which gold cracked letters spelled an aged "M-A-R-I-N-E."

"So what're you reading there, Professor?" asked Hatch.

"*Seven Pillars of Wisdom*," I replied, "by T. E. Lawrence."

"He translated Homer and shit," said Phalen, "d'you know that, Gunny?"

"No, guess I didn't. Is one of them pillars 'Never be a company gunny?'"

The gunny went next door to talk with the captain, then call around to the other bases for information. Hatch and Phalen returned to their tents for sleep. I picked up Lawrence again:

> And it came upon me freshly how the secret of uniform was to make a crowd solid, dignified, impersonal: to give it the singleness and tautness of an upstanding man. This death's livery which walled its bearers from ordinary life, was sign that they had sold their wills and bodies to the State: and contracted themselves into a service not the less abject for that its beginning was voluntary. Some of them had obeyed the instinct of lawless-

ness: some were hungry: others thirsted for glamour, for the supposed colour of a military life: but of them all, those only received satisfaction who had sought to degrade themselves, for to the peace-eye they were below humanity.

In the night's silence, I pondered the century-old Soldier's Tale, part of which I wanted to tell. I half-hoped that the white Toyota would crash the gates and begin firing from behind the plywood outhouses into the company office tent. I did not notice his entrance, but Gunny Benson stood alone in the doorway before me.

"Mind if I come in?" he asked.

"By all means. Is everything worked out with the ammunition?"

"Fuck if I know, I couldn't get a hold of no-goddam-body. You know, *most* people sleepin' at four in the mornin.'"

I sighed. "I suppose we'll be home in our own beds soon enough. Don't you think?"

"Yeah? Soon enough ain't soon enough for me. Give me another one of them cigarettes, would you, Professor?"

I handed him a Camel, and began to talk, but he waved me off while reaching for my lighter.

"Professor," he asked, "what do you think's gonna happen to this place after we leave?"

"This camp, or the Middle East?"

"The Middle-fuckin'-East," he said. "You think they'll get rid of Saddam? I mean, his own people?"

"I don't know," I said, "I doubt it. It's interesting, really, to look back at the struggles Lawrence went through during the First World War— ending in nothing more noble than a corrupt balance of power, just as this one."

"We're doomed to repeat it, right?" said the gunny. "It's true. Most people don't even bother to look around 'em, and if they do, they're too afraid to point the finger at the man they see oppressin' 'em. People just don't learn, Professor. Got heads thicker than a Kevlar fuckin' helmet."

I held a cigarette out without lighting it. "You know, Gunny, a friend of mine and I like to say that the difference between a wise man and a fool is that the wise man will have twenty years' experience, and a fool one year's experience twenty times over."

The gunny sat silently, watching me light my cigarette. He looked down for a second, then smiled. "You talk like that with the boys in the Pound? You did, I know it. Worse thing is, they *listened* to that shit. Hell, I can't even get 'em to listen to the simple shit I tell 'em in formation, and I'm their *gunny*."

"Maybe," I said whitely, heavy on the nasal, "you should learn to break the shit down to 'em, you know, work it a little."

Life in the Dog Pound flashed through my mind after that sentence: jawin' with Ebbers and Farmer and Hatch, out stealing shit from the Army with the Rat, talking psychology and literature with Riley, arguing with Bones about racism . . . and now I would never see them again. After the war, Hatch would be just another black man struggling to make a life in North Philly, and so would Ebbers and Farmer. Bones would be teaching and coaching wrestling in Delaware. Riley would be doing grad school at Temple. I would no longer be the Professor, but just another philosophy major at the University of Minnesota.

Gunny Benson laughed, then raised himself in his chair, head rocking gently in dismay. "Turnipseed? You one fucked-up character."

In the silence that followed his laughter, I poured another bottle of water into the canteen, then struck a match to the Bunsen burner.

"You really dig that philosophy, huh? It's your *passion*, right?"

"Yeah, I suppose it is," I replied. "Passion—that's a good word, isn't it?"

"It is. But nobody gives a shit 'bout anything anymore, Professor. You heard of Dick Gregory?"

"No, I haven't," I answered.

"He's a hero of mine. I bet you didn't think I had heroes, huh? That's right—Dick Gregory. I once heard him say, 'There will come a day in America when there will be no education, only indoctrination; when

Human Rights have been supplanted by Property Rights'—what do you think of *that*, Professor?"

"I think the day has come."

"That's right. I heard Gregory say that after I got back from 'Nam. I said the same thing right then: Brother, that day's already here."

"I didn't think you'd be such a radical, Gunny."

"Black man gotta be a radical, Professor. Gregory, he taught me that. He was a talkin' motherfucker just like your ass. You'll be a radical, too— a funky-ass fuckin' radical, Professor."

"We'll see about *that*. I'm done being a radical, Gunny. But I can't tell you how happy I am to see a Marine Corps gunnery sergeant quoting a black radical. Really, this is one of the highlights of my career."

In the same nasal tone in which the Pound had made so much fun of me, the gunny replied, "Yes, well, actually, it is not so very frequently that one sits in the company of a white-ass little professor from Minne-fuck-ing-apolis in the middle of war in the motherfucking desert."

The gunny reached for another cigarette. "You know somethin', Turnipseed? I'm so damned happy we're sittin' around bullshittin' like this, you know, that me and you ain't all fucked up right now. I ain't very religious, but I prayed like a motherfucker that none of my boys in the Pound would get hurt. Like a God-fearin' motherfucker."

He took a deep breath.

"And for you all over at Minneapolis, that musta been tough to lose Corporal Joseph."

"Yeah, that was tough," I said. "But you know something? I mean, I really don't understand it, but I didn't really care when he died. I didn't even go to the service. But then, the other day, when I went to the memorial service for a guy I didn't even know, I just about cried. They played 'Eternal Father,' and the Marine Corps Hymn, and I just about lost it."

"Yeah, that's tough. You never know what you're gonna feel when shit happens. I know that sure enough . . ."

A jungle smell rose in the tent, and the subject of Vietnam surrounded the gunny's broken silence.

"Ain't nothin' like 'Nam though. That was some shit to figure out. We were kids younger than you, seein' shit . . . Patrols, firefights, even the streets of Saigon. Everybody was sub-fuckin'-humanized, Professor. You know there's shit can kill you without even touchin' you?"

He paused. The canteen of water was bubbling away as I looked down at the cigarette ashes spilled over his toes and flip-flops. The captain in the dispatch tent was barking at one of the WMS about fucked-up paperwork. Trip tickets.

"In 'Nam, we had these two new kids assigned to my platoon, you know, these dudes practically ain't shavin' yet. Word came down on their first day—out into the boonies. So we went out on a patrol with the fuckin' new guys, two of 'em. Jesus. These two lost it on their first fuckin' day. I think one of 'em permanent. We came through the bush out into this little ville, this ville had already been burnt right down to ashes, which I had seen before, right? But not on my first patrol. That's a motherfucker. And then we kinda made out at the head of the road comin' into the ville, which we didn't take 'cause we came through the ass-end, and the vc had set up a kind of terror for us. These two girls had been nailed up to some posts. These girls had been *crucified*—and you know, Professor, they had been *pregnant*, their little babies cut right out of their bellies and let hang out onto the ground. All the fuckin' intestines and shit was still movin' like they was *alive,* and them babies had that shit, maggots and worms, all crawlin' out of their heads. Two little girls and their babies, sacrificed like Vietnamese Jesuses. Just hanging there with their heads turned down, crying maggots onto the dirt. It was too much for *me,* and I was on my second tour. I said right then, 'Benson, you got to get your ass out this place—just get the fuck out.' An' the one of them kids, he just started pukin' his brains out, and cryin' and spittin' all over himself and . . . and then he would just sit and stare at them girls, lookin' out at 'em with that fuckin' stare, right? We had to carry that motherfucker out of there. Just up and carried his ass out, 'cuz he was already dead. He was breathin' all right, but he was already fuckin' dead."

"And now *we're* heroes," I said. "Isn't that some fucked-up shit?"

"Naw, it ain't fucked up, Professor. You all worked your ass off, and you didn't know comin' in here that you wouldn't get your asses blown up. Shit, we got something like three dead in our battalion itself—coulda just as well been your dead ass."

"'Nam, though. What the fuck it must have been like to come home from that shit."

"Yeah, Professor, now that was some sad-ass shit. Some stereotypical sad-ass shit, just like in the movies. You went home alone after 'Nam. I didn't have nobody to talk to, you know, like you and me are doing right here, I didn't have nobody after 'Nam. So you know, when I get back from this shit, shit like this you see all the time, every day, and I get back and take the train up to Philly from Quantico and all I want to do is see my family, which ain't much any-damned-way, but that's okay, cause I just want to see some-fuckin'-body ain't been killin' people, I want to see somebody still got love in 'em, you know, maybe some of that shit gonna rub back off onto me. Oh no, not Benson, he ain't done with the war yet, he gonna get it right up the ass one more time for good measure. I'm comin' up them stairs in Thirtieth Street Station, and this little girl, beautiful in one of them lacy dresses, like an angel of the Lord herself, comes runnin' up to me with a big ol' smile when I say 'Hello, sweet girl' to her, and you know, her fuckin' cunt mother calls out after her, 'Hey now, darlin', don't go near *that* man.'"

Nothing in the tent moved but the smoke rising in quiet whorls from our cigarettes.

"I just 'bout lost it. I really did. The whole war I survived without losin' it, but when that fuckin' cunt said that shit, well now . . . Turnipseed, you can't trust nobody's intentions but your own. Your own and the people you love. You gotta have people you love. You don't have people you love, you don't know who the fuck to listen to when you start goin' crazy. I'd a fuckin' killt somebody's ass that mornin', Turnipseed, if it hadn't been for an old World War II vet who was lining up drinks for me. Yeah, if it weren't for his loving ass, I'd a just up and fuckin' killt somebody. I *know* I woulda, 'cuz I didn't give a fat flyin' fuck 'bout nothin', people gonna treat me like that. What kind of fuckin' emotion am I supposed to feel then? I don't fuckin' know. I ain't ever gonna know about those days, they were too fuckin' crazy. If nobody loves you, Professor, you ain't got shit to base the world on—I may be a dumbfuck ol' gunny, but I learned that much."

A long silence passed, and each of us wiped a tear from the corner of our eye. When he spoke again, it was with a fresh voice, tired, but renewed.

"You'd think that people would sooner or later get it right, Professor," he said, "you know, stop livin' like assholes. Instead, they keep doin' the same old stupid shit. Maybe you oughta come up with a Word of the Day for that one."

"Maybe I should."

"Me? I'm goin' to educate every-fuckin'-body I see. Shit, I don't care if they argue with my black old ass, 'cause maybe that way *one* of us is going to learn something."

Gunny Benson was standing up now, looking over at the tent flaps, at the pale blue sky between them.

"Well, Turnipseed—Professor—I'm goin' to try and get some sleep before I have to call formation. You go ahead and keep on skatin' in here, I'll take care of it. You hooked up with me, hear? You just promise me you goin' to keep reading them books. Remember—you got to fuck with people every chance you get, make 'em argue so much they start to think."

After the gunny left, I returned to Lawrence, who brought me through till morning:

The irony was in my loving objects before life or ideas; the incongruity in my answering the infectious call of action, which laid weight on the diversity of things. It was a hard task for me to straddle feeling and action. I had had one craving all my life—for the power of self-expression in some imaginative form—but had been too diffuse ever to acquire technique. At last accident, with perverted humour, in casting me as a man of action had given me a place in the Arab Revolt . . . The epic mode was alien to me, as to my generation. Memory gave me no clue to the heroic, so that I could not feel such men as Auda in myself. He seemed fantastic as the hills of Rumm, old as Mallory.

"Is that right, Burgess? Well, you're gonna go relieve him right now. SULLIVAN!"

"Here."

When all men and all things were accounted for, myself included, we boarded the buses for the airport. I pressed my cheek against the window, looking out at the refineries. They were no longer drip-riddled candles on God's drafting tables, but landmarks on the highway into the port area. Indeed, they were no longer refineries, but gas-oil separation facilities, which we now recognized. Now I was riding past them for the last time.

Early in the morning we arrived at Jubayl Naval Airport. Its windows were no longer boarded with plywood, but sparkled with dew. The sidewalks had just recently been poured, and the brick facade was still spotted with cement chunks from its construction. Inside they had installed several video games and a fast-food counter. Televisions hung from brackets high in the corners, and we watched CNN: sports, Hollywood, the markets. A fashion minute. We were still at war, but the rest of the world had already moved on. We stared dryly at the TVs.

When our plane arrived, we watched it taxi down the runway.

"Okay, everyone! Get on your gear! Let's form it up!"

Calls rang out from the Staff NCOs, ordering their troops onto the tarmac for formation. The wind was strong, and the ear-piercing sound of the turbines roused us further. We stood shoulder to shoulder, caps held against our chests, as proud as we had ever been in our lives, and as expectant. We were only two ranks deep, and I looked across my left shoulder down a row of more than a hundred men: ugly, handsome, smart and dumb, tall and short and all proud to be Americans. We stood together: mechanics and drivers and engineers, soon to be teachers, accountants, farmers, and salesmen again.

"Awright, listen up: File it off from the first rank! Let's go! Let's go!"

A deafening fanfare from the common man rose up. Our collective

Semper Fidelis

I WAS STILL ON NIGHT DUTY when the buses pulled in to take us to the customs warehouse. There they would shake us down, emptying our seabags and inspecting our pockets. I had just gotten in from a long walk and a cigarette when I heard the air brakes on the buses from up at the camp gates. I was finishing a journal entry when they screeched to a halt in front of the tent next door, the dispatch office, and mine, the company office.

I stepped out of the tent, leaning against the tent frame. I stood in silence, watching and smoking a cigarette. Men were heaving seabags onto the beds of five-tons, working in the headlights of the truck behind. Flashlights and headlights wove their beams through the rising dust. Rifle boxes were padlocked and stacked on a separate truck. ALICE packs and athletic bags and knapsacks had been stashed up against the wall of tents where their owners could find them to carry onto the bus. Formations of men began to take shape out of the chaos.

"QUINONES!"

"Here."

"Good. RICARDO?"

"Here."

"SALERNO! Where's Salerno!"

"He's staying in country, Gunny," someone answered.

"SAUNDERS!"

"He's on a workin' party."

"No shit, Gunny, you just sent him a half-hour ago." Everyone laughed.

boots shook the tarmac. I was fourth in line, and stumbled with joy. We paused below the aluminum stairs rising up to the plane, and beamed at the captain and stewardess waiting for us at the top, waving small American flags. I was dizzy. Unabashed, a tear came to my eye, a swelling of pride. I climbed the stairs, past the clean broad shoulders of the captain and the lusty perfume of the stewardess.

Sarah never wrote. The war and the media circus of CNN were too much for her already frail sense of self. She was diagnosed as having literally lost her Self. She could no longer connect her thoughts to her body. She stopped eating altogether. Stopped going home. Mary found her one day, at a bus stop in St. Paul near the house on Summit Avenue at which Mary had rented Sarah a room. She weighed less than seventy pounds. When I saw her in the hospital afterwards—the last time I ever saw her—it occurred to me that she was even more emaciated than the Iraqi POWs.

When we touched down at Norton Air Force Base, we were exhausted. It was almost midnight, and we gathered in a damp hangar after deplaning. The smell of coffee burned like acid through the damp, and I looked over to see two verdigris-encrusted percolators. A defunct vending machine stood next to them, by the chipped doors of the restrooms.

"Okay, gentlemen," called the broken-nosed captain from Dallas, "before we board the buses back to Pendleton, Staff Sergeant Grey—Boomer—is gonna give you a little talk on behalf of those of us who fought in our last war."

The captain's nose took on a beauty in its ugliness, and we all stood stock-still, shivers frozen, as Boomer took center stage. Behind him were the captain, and Gunny Benson, and a couple other guys I never really got to know: men in their forties, with grey stubble on their hard chins, bags beneath their eyes, and rounded stomachs pressing against their camouflage.

Boomer's voice was hoarse even as he began.

"I ain't gonna stand up here and fiddle-fuck around," he said, "'cuz I want to get you gentlemen—and ladies—out onto the bus and back to Pendleton. The airmen here tell me you guys are going to get one hell of a reception on your way out of here. A real live tit-swingin' hero's welcome. Now . . ."

He paused then looked back at the half-dozen men behind him. Gunny Benson cracked a small smile and nodded. So did the captain. And the other men. Each of them leaned back a little, at parade rest.

"Now . . . I want you gentlemen to eat this up, really take it in, every fuckin' second. Every half-second. These crazy folks are going to be cheering for you guys like you're the greatest American heroes that ever lived. And you deserve it. Even if you don't feel like you deserve it, you do. The Baghdad Express hauled more ammunition than any other motor transport battalion in Marine Corps history. That's you, gentlemen. We had a few casualties. A few deaths. Any of those could have been any of you. Believe it, gentlemen, you're heroes."

He stopped to let his words sink in. The airmen standing behind Boomer and the Vietnam vets looked small, young, and embarrassed. My chest ached, and I could feel the forward and backward bob of my body with each throbbing pulse.

"The reason, gentlemen—and ladies—*Marines*. The reason I'm up here, with all these old farts behind me, is us Vietnam vets wanted to tell you just how special this moment is going to be, and help you all to experience it in the proper fashion. None of us can ever really feel like a hero. Look at us, we're all a little bit old, and a lotta bit broken. That reception out there, no matter if the ladies have double-dee swingin' tits, or how many flags are waving, or how many cases of cold beer they pass our way, they can never give us back the reception we missed. We had our war, and we can't have it back. Now you Marines have had yours, and you came home heroes. Be proud . . . and remember."

An adamantine trust in truth and right. Plato knew that this was a fragile trust, for his fellow Greek, Homer, wrote the horror of its breach in the *Iliad*. When Agamemnon stole Achilles' prize, he also stole Achilles' trust, and, in turn, destroyed his character. That a broken trust can ruin a man is as old as truths get. That a man can rid himself of the need for trust is philosophy's first calling. The conflict between these two understandings—or the acceptance of the one and the striving for the other—is the basis of what Plato two and a half millennia ago called the "Ancient Quarrel."

And how would we have known, standing in the shadows of Boomer and Benson, that we would have our turn at unease and untruth. That we would not be making jokes about Agent Orange, but clinical studies of PB, anthrax vaccines, depleted uranium, smoke, pesticides . . . wondering, in the wake of Gulf War Syndrome and lingering doubts about the purpose of our war, what role our trust in our government, our society, our leaders, has in the task of instilling trust in ourselves.

We piled onto the green Marine Corps school buses like we were headed for another war. Whispers, at most, broke the silence and the night hung dark and low behind the magnesium halos of the base lights. The buses coasted over the tarmac, then onto the service road heading for the gate. Windows slapped down to let out the fog of bodies hot with anticipation. The headlights of the first bus swung across the gates, lighting up hundreds of faces. Chrome from dozens of cars and trucks sparkled, and the first audible murmurs of the crowd pulsed through the hushed aisles of our bus. Two Air Force MPs opened the gates, and we rolled into a bacchanalian dream: women with breasts painted with stars, hundreds of fireworks shooting into the sky, at our bus, bouncing off, then exploding in bouncing sparks along the road; faces of fat men and skinny children pushed up against the windows of the bus, screaming; cars not by the dozen but by the hundred with their tailgating owners barbecuing and drinking; signs of every size, from small flag to van-side banners proclaimed us HEROES!

The first beer grenade went off near where I was sitting: a red and white cannister of highly-charged Budweiser. Then one burst against a window. It was total mayhem, with guys diving everywhere. When I looked behind me, someone had opened the emergency door. Sprinting behind us as fast as he could run, a balding man heaved a case of Budweiser into the back of the bus. It crushed against the door-frame, sending more foam spraying in every direction. Bergman was first to throw himself onto the case, then Heinemann. Out from the frothy mess of men and beer, a fist thrust toward my face:

"Turnipseed, a lukewarm Budweiser. Whadda ya say?"

I said, "Thanks!" and took the can, spraying half of it up my nose— deliriously enjoying the rest.

I felt like I had lost my mind. And found two more. I stayed up all night with Boomer and the guys, drinking at the E-Club, which they kept open for us. We put our last drinks down fifteen minutes before morning formation, then stood tall smelling like beer and piss and wearing two-day beards. I found this a fine state of affairs. In the afternoon, I went to the PX, where I found Ray Monk's new biography of Wittgenstein. This and Marquez's *The General in His Labyrinth,* about Simón Bolívar. I never imagined that a PX carried such things. It was like a new world had come into being, where I could simultaneously be a nasty drunk Marine and a philosopher manqué.

These were strange, lazy days. I grew impatient. And, weirdly, confident—as though I had passed some invisible boundary; that certain things, previously contradictory, didn't have to matter much anymore.

It's hard to explain, this new sense, but it can be summed up in an incident that would sound made up if it weren't true: the day I dressed down a brigadier general. The whole time we were at Pendleton, no one had told us when we were going home. We had nothing to do. So we had liberty all day, every day, except for morning and afternoon formation. We had ninety-sixes almost every weekend. After several weeks of this, we were marched to a baseball diamond and told to file into a bleacher: the head of the Fourth Marine Air Wing is in town and he's going to give us a speech. So the brigadier general came in with his gaggle of colonels and first lieutenants and gave his speech. We're the Baghdad Express.

We moved more ammo than God. Then moved it back again. We're big heroes. He mentions no word of going home. Then he asks us if we have any questions.

One guy gets up and asks, "Sir, is it true that we're up for a meritorious unit citation?"

"Well, Marine. I've heard great things about the Sixth Motor Transport Battalion—all you men and women of Saudi Motors and the Baghdad Express. You're legends. If justice is served, someone's writing up paperwork right now to recommend you."

The crowd buzzed for a moment, then fell silent. We knew right then there were no special medals for us—we were truck-driving reservists.

"Do any other Marines have a question?"

I stood up.

"Yeah, I have a question."

One of the officers standing next to the general yelled out, "Sir!"

"Yeah," I said, "my question is: 'When will people stop blowing smoke up our ass and tell us when we're going home?"

"Sir!"

The general couldn't fucking believe himself.

"Marine," he declared, "I suggest that if someone has done you wrong, you report that fact up the chain of command."

"But I'm not talking about me, I'm talking about, you know: people are missing out on paychecks, spring planting on their farms, engineering projects, their kids' baseball league sign-up, sex with their wives. And all we do is sit around all day buying Cheetos and Gatorade at the PX with our shitty paychecks. Oh, and stand in formation. So, like, when are we going home?"

I have to hand it to him, he definitely had the "no bad days" principle of leadership down, because he left us with a big, cool hookah enema.

"You Marines are heroes. You put it on the line for your country and your Corps. You give it honor. When your noble sacrifice is through, you will be reunited with your families and friends and neighbors. Semper Fidelis, Marines."

Right face, get the fuck out of here. When he was gone, our major turned to one of his captains, one of the guys from Dallas, then called me down out of the stands.

"Turnipseed! Get your ass down here."

You wouldn't believe it, all the hell we gave each other, but the guys in the bleachers gave me a standing fucking ovation. And that was that. No punishment, no grief—just the recognition that, for once, we were all in the same shit together.

Now, on hot summer afternoons in Minneapolis, when they test the civil defense sirens, they also call my attention, like a muezzin calling prayer, asking me to face toward Mecca or a few hundred miles beyond, toward places I'd never heard of before: Kibrit, Mishab, Khafji, and Jubayl; toward the place where I gave up the desire for the otherworldly perfection philosophy demanded of me and embraced the shadows. Shadows like the ones cast by trees swaying in the breeze, or by ten-year-old girls with cornrows and endless rhymes, endless enthusiasms, or the long shadows of late June evenings cast by a writer who used to be a Marine. And I will spend a lifetime trying to explain the complex of emotions— anger, pride, love, honor, ambiguity, betrayal, and hope—that inhere in the motto *Semper Fidelis:* Always Faithful.

"THE MOST BEAUTIFUL WORLD IS LIKE A HEAP OF RUBBLE, THROWN DOWN IN CONFUSION."

HERACLITUS' LAST FRAGMENT (DK 124)

Acknowledgments

I WOULD LIKE TO THANK, first and foremost, Professor John M. Dolan. His high standards for both intellect and virtue I will be hard-pressed to live up to; his generosity and patience with me in my many and various wayward enterprises have been priceless. I wouldn't be who I am if not for him. To my wife, Lyra Hernandez: you hang the stars out for me every night. To those who taught me how to write, and be a writer, a huge hand: Trish Hampl, Mimi Sprengnether, Bill Kittredge, Tom Mallon, Robert Bly, Alec Wilkinson, Jane Brox. Special notice to my great friends Joseph Clark and Aliki Barnstone—you are treasures of art and friendship. To the institutions that recognized and rewarded me as I struggled: The Loft, the Bread Loaf Writers' Conference, and the Minnesota State Arts Board—I'm forever grateful. To those who published me: *Blue Moon Quarterly, Two Cities,* and GQ—your confidence in me made this book possible. Special thanks to Ilena Silverman, who taught me that it is possible to write a great piece—and that you can make it through the hell it takes to get there: for me, she wrote the map. Ted Genoways, my editor, and the rest of the folks at Borealis Books deserve thanks for giving me the opportunity to go off and see an entirely different species of elephant. The enthusiasm and energy of Brooke Fitzsimmons made the grueling bearable (and the fun possible). The generosity and tenacity of Melissa Flashman and Ellen Levine at Trident Media give me an undeserved confidence; a secret weapon. Working with Hilary Redmon on the paperback was not only an honor, but a treat: in addition to possessing a great wit, her editorial eye gleams like blue steel. I'm a lucky writer for having all these great folks in my corner. Brian Kelly deserves huge thanks for his work on the illustrations—you rock, pal. And the last to whom I'll grovel and offer props—the friends, family, and readers who stood by all these years and taught me how to be human with good grace and good laughs, despite the pain: Dave and Maggie Knutson, Mark and Mary Durfee, Andy and Debby Cox, Paul and Jess Fischer, Kevin Fenton and Ellen Shaffer, Chi-Ting Huang, Flo Wu, Dave Dikeman, Matt Gould, Scott Sanders, Francis J. Lu, David Olson, Diane Palmquist, Jason Scherschligt, Dan Carr, Reverend Ray McDaniel, Jen Yasis, Niels Strandskov, my bro' Mike Turnipseed, my grandparents John and Merna Maher, and, it just wouldn't be right—the crew at the Village Wok, 2530, and the boys from the Dog Pound. I give it up to all of you.